SPECTRUM®

Geometry

Grade 6

D1225322

Spectrum®
An imprint of Carson-Dellosa Publishing LLC
P.O. Box 35665
Greensboro, NC 27425 USA

© 2014 Carson-Dellosa Publishing LLC. Except as permitted under the United States Copyright Act, no part of this publication may be reproduced, stored, or distributed in any form or by any means (mechanically, electronically, recording, etc.) without the prior written consent of Carson-Dellosa Publishing LLC. Spectrum® is an imprint of Carson-Dellosa Publishing LLC.

Printed in the USA • All rights reserved.   ISBN 978-1-4838-0481-1

04-243151151

Table of Contents Grade 6

Spectrum Geometry is designed to build a solid foundation in geometry for your sixth grader. Aligned to the sixth grade Common Core State Standards for geometry, every page equips your child with the confidence to master geometry. Helpful examples provide step-by-step guidance to teach new concepts, followed by a variety of practice pages that will sharpen your child's skills and efficiency at problem solving. Use the Pretests, Posttests, Mid-Test, and Final Test as the perfect way to track your child's progress and identify where he or she needs extra practice.

Common Core State Standards Alignment: Geometry Grade 6

Domain: The Number System	
Standard	Aligned Practice Pages
6.NS.6a	69–70
6.NS.6b	72–76
6.NS.6c	69, 71–76, 78–79
6.NS.8	69, 71–76, 78–79
Domain: Geometry	
Standard	Aligned Practice Pages
6.G.1	42, 46–50, 57, 58, 61, 68, 64, 78, 81–82
6.G.2	42, 53–57, 65–66, 68, 79, 80–82
6.G.3	73–74, 78–79
6.G.4	42, 51–52, 58, 62–63, 68, 79, 82

* © Copyright 2010. National Governors Association Center for Best Practices and Council of Chief State School Officers. All rights reserved.

Check What You Know

Points, Lines, Rays, and Angles

Under each of the following items, write line, line segment, or ray. Then, circle the correct names. Each may have more than one correct name.

1.

   a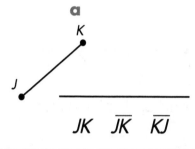

_____

$\overline{JK}$ $\overline{JK}$ $\overline{KJ}$

   b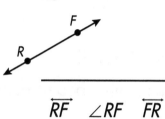

_____

$\overrightarrow{RF}$ $\angle RF$ $\overrightarrow{FR}$

   c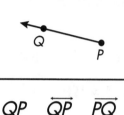

_____

QP $\overleftrightarrow{QP}$ $\overline{PQ}$

Name the angles that have L as their vertex.

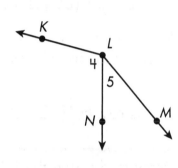

2. _____ _____ _____

Name ∠5 in two different ways.

3. _____ _____

Use the figure to complete the following.

4. Name an angle that is vertical to ∠ABD. _____

5. Name an angle that is vertical to ∠GBH. _____

6. Name an angle that is supplementary

to ∠EBC. _____

7. ∠EBC is 90°. $\overrightarrow{BF}$ bisects ∠EBC.

What is the measure of ∠EBF? _____

8. Name the angle that is complementary to ∠FBC. _____

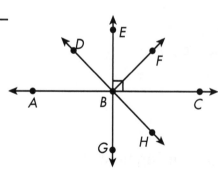

SCORE ⬭ / 8

Points, Lines, and Rays

A **point** has no dimensions but defines a location in space.

Points are usually named by the capital letter. *A•*

A **line** extends infinitely in both directions.

A line is named by choosing any two points on a line.

Line *BC* ($\overleftrightarrow{BC}$) is the same as line *CB* ($\overleftrightarrow{CB}$).

A **line segment** is part of a line that begins at one point and ends at another.

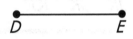

Segment *DE* ($\overline{DE}$) is the same as segment *ED* ($\overline{ED}$).

A **ray** is an infinitely long part of a line that begins at a point called a *vertex*. To name a ray, choose another point on the ray and name it from its vertex.

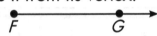

This is ray *FG* ($\overrightarrow{FG}$). It is not ray *GF* because *G* is not its vertex.

Draw and name the following figures.

1. line *AB*   •*A*   •*B*   _____

2. ray *FG*   •*F*   •*G*   _____

3. line segment *HK*   •*H*   •*K*   _____

4. line segment *KH*   •*H*   •*K*   _____

Points and Lines

Complete the following.

	a	**b**
1.	line RS or SR	$\overrightarrow{RS}$ or $\overleftarrow{SR}$
2.	line _____ or _____	_____ or _____
3.	line _____ or _____	_____ or _____

	a	**b**	**c**
4.	line segment XY or ___	$\overline{XY}$ or ___	endpoints ___ and ___
5.	line segment ___ or ___	___ or ___	endpoints ___ and ___

Draw the following.

	a	**b**
6.	line TU	$\overrightarrow{OP}$
7.	$\overline{GH}$	$\overrightarrow{JK}$
8.	line segment XY	$\overline{WX}$

Measuring Angles

An **angle** (∠) is formed by two rays which have a common vertex.

The angle is named *ABC* (∠*ABC*) or *CBA* (∠*CBA*). The **vertex**, the point where two rays meet, is always in the middle of the angle name. The measure of ∠*ABC* is 45°.

If the measure of an angle is less than 90°, it is an acute angle.	If the measure of an angle is 90°, it is a right angle.	If the measure of an angle is more than 90°, it is an obtuse angle.
	This symbol means right angle. 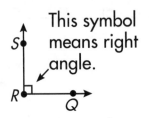	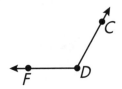
This angle (∠) is formed by $\overrightarrow{BA}$ and $\overrightarrow{BC}$.	∠*QRS* is a right angle.	∠*CDF* is obtuse. The measure of ∠*CDF* is 117°.

Name each angle. Write whether it is acute (A), right (R), or obtuse (O). Then, measure the angle.

1.

_____

_____

_____

2.

_____

_____

_____

3.

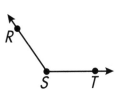

_____

_____

_____

SCORE ⬭ / 4

Types of Angles

Vertical angles are formed when two straight lines intersect. They are opposite angles and are equal in measure. ∠A and ∠C are a pair of vertical angles. ∠B and ∠D are also vertical angles.

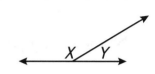

Two angles are **supplementary** if their sum is 180°. In the figure, ∠X and ∠Y are supplementary angles. The measure of ∠X = 150° and the measure of ∠Y = 30°. If two angles have a common vertex and their sides form a straight line, they are supplementary because a straight line has an angle measure of 180°.

Two angles are **complementary** if their sum is 90°. In the figure, ∠M and ∠N are complementary. The measure of ∠M is 40° and the measure of ∠N is 50°.

An **angle bisector** is a line drawn through the vertex of an angle that divides it into two congruent angles, or angles that have the same measure. In the figure, ray BD bisects ∠ABC so that the measure of ∠ABD is the same as the measure of ∠DBC.

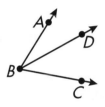

Solve each problem.

1. ∠A and ∠G are vertical angles. The measure of ∠A is 72°, what is the measure of ∠G? _____

2. ∠Y and ∠Z are supplementary angles. The measure of ∠Y is 112°. What is the measure of ∠Z? _____

3. ∠A and ∠B are complementary angles. The measure of ∠A is 53°. What is the measure of ∠B? _____

4. ∠RST is bisected by ray SW. The measure of ∠WST is 30°, what is the measure of ∠RST? _____

SCORE ◯ / 10

Vertical, Supplementary, and Complementary Angles

Use the figure at the right to answer questions 1–4.

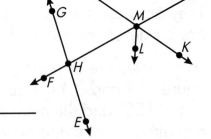

1. Name an angle that is vertical to ∠EHF.   _____

2. Name an angle that is vertical to ∠EHM.   _____

3. Name an angle that is supplementary to ∠IMJ.   _____

4. Name the bisector of ∠HMK.   _____

Use the figure at the right to answer questions 5 and 6.

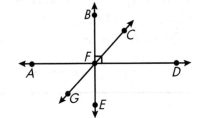

5. Name an angle complementary to ∠BFC.   _____

6. Name an angle complementary to ∠AFG.   _____

Solve.

7. ∠RST is supplementary to angle ∠PSO. The measure of ∠RST is 103°.

   What is the measure of ∠PSO?   _____

8. ∠MNO and ∠NOP are complementary. The measure of ∠NOP is 22°.

   What is the measure of ∠MNO?   _____

9. ∠XYZ is bisected by $\overrightarrow{YW}$. The measure of ∠XYW is 52°. What is the measure of ∠WYZ? What is the measure of ∠XYZ?

   The measure of ∠WYZ is   _____

   The measure of ∠XYZ is   _____

Rays and Angles

Complete the following.

	a	**b**

1.  ray *AB* or $\overrightarrow{AB}$ endpoint *A*

2.  ray _____ _____ endpoint _____

3. ray _____ _____ endpoint _____

4. angle *GHI* or *IHG* ∠*GHI* or ∠*IHG*

ray $\overrightarrow{HG}$ or $\overrightarrow{HI}$ vertex *H*

5.  angle _____ or _____ _____ or _____

rays _____ and _____ vertex _____

6. angle _____ or _____ _____ or _____

rays _____ and _____ vertex _____

Use the points to draw the following.

	a	**b**

7. $\overrightarrow{XY}$ •Y •X $\overline{TU}$ •T •U

8. ∠*RST* R• S• •T ∠*PQR* R• •Q •P

Check What You Learned

Points, Lines, Rays, and Angles

CHAPTER 1 POSTTEST

Under each of the following items, write *line*, *line segment*, or *ray*. Then, circle the correct names. Each has more than one correct name.

1.   a   b   c

_____   _____   _____

$\overleftrightarrow{ED}$ $\overleftrightarrow{DE}$ $\overrightarrow{DE}$ DE   AB BA $\overline{AB}$ $\overline{BA}$ KM MK $\overrightarrow{MK}$ ∠MK

Name the angles that have *P* as their vertex.

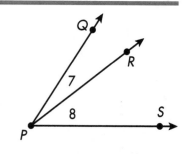

2. _____ _____ _____

Name ∠8 in two different ways.

3. _____ _____

Use the figure to answer the following.

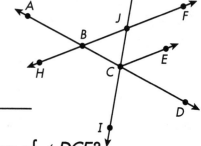

4. Name an angle that is vertical to ∠BJC. _____

5. Name an angle that is vertical to ∠ACG. _____

6. Name an angle that is supplementary to ∠JCD. _____

7. ∠DCJ is 90°. $\overrightarrow{CE}$ bisects ∠DCJ. What is the angle measure of ∠DCE? _____

8. Name an angle that is complementary to ∠DCE. _____

Check What You Know

Problem Solving: Points, Lines, Rays, and Angles

Read the problem carefully and solve. Show your work under each question.

Dennis plans to remodel his backyard. He draws a model of the yard on graph paper. He labels his drawing and uses a ruler to make straight lines.

---

1. Dennis wants to put a pool in his backyard. He draws a line segment to show one side of the pool. Draw and name line segment *CD* below.

2. Dennis draws the figure below. Identify and name this figure.

_____   _____

3. Dennis draws a right angle to show a corner of his yard. He names the angle *IJK*. Draw and label ∠*IJK* in the space below.

4. Dennis draws the angle below to show a part of his patio. Name the angle, and write whether it is obtuse, acute, or right.

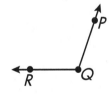

_____   _____

Rays and Angles

Read the problem carefully and solve. Show your work under each question.

Alvin is helping to plan a playground for the neighborhood. The playground plan has many rays and angles.

> **Helpful Hint**
>
> An angle is the union of two rays. The middle of the angle is where the two rays meet.

1. One corner of the playground is represented using the angle shown below. Use geometric notation to name the angle in two ways.

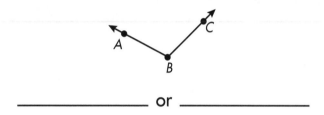

_____ or _____

2. Alvin draws a ray on the plan that shows the direction people will enter the playground. How would he label ray *MN* on the plans?

_____

Rays and Angles

3. Alvin combined two rays, $\overrightarrow{BA}$ and $\overrightarrow{BC}$, to make an angle at the edge of the playground plan. Draw and label this angle.

_____

4. Alvin was asked to draw angle *RQS* to represent the relationship of the slide to the ground. He drew the angle shown below. Did Alvin draw the angle correctly?

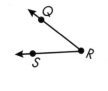

_____

5. The gate and the fence in the playground form the angle shown below. Name two geometric figures that are combined to make this angle?

_____

Types of Angles

Read the problem carefully and solve. Show your work under each question.

Keisha makes a map of the streets near her house. She uses angles and intersecting lines to represent the streets. She decides to label the lines and angles on her map. She also plans to measure some of the angles.

Helpful Hint

Vertical angles are formed when two straight lines intersect. They are opposite angles and are equal.

Two angles are **supplementary** if their sum is 180°.

Two angles are **complementary** if their sum is 90°.

An **angle bisector** is a line drawn through the vertex of an angle that divides it into two angles that have the same measure.

---

1. Keisha measures two supplementary angles, $\angle J$ and $\angle K$, on her map. The measure of $\angle K$ is 124°. What is the measure of $\angle J$?

_____

2. Keisha draws $\angle RST$ below. She draws $\overrightarrow{SV}$ so that it bisects $\angle RST$. The measure of $\angle VST$ is 25°. What is the measure of $\angle RST$?

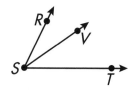

_____

Types of Angles

Use the figure below for questions 3 and 4.

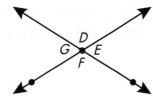

3. Keisha draws the pair of lines above to show the intersection of two streets. Identify ∠D and ∠F as supplementary, complementary, or vertical.

_____

4. In Keisha's drawing above, identify ∠F and ∠G as supplementary, complementary, or vertical.

_____

5. Keisha measures two complementary angles, ∠B and ∠C, on her map. The measure of ∠B is 35°. What is the measure of ∠C?

_____

Vertical, Supplementary, and Complementary Angles

Read the problem carefully and solve. Show your work under each question.

Chang uses lines and angles to create a map of the streets near his home. The map is represented by the drawing to the right.

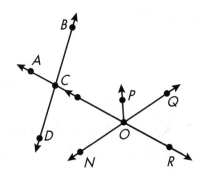

1. Chang has a friend who lives at the corner represented by ∠BCO. Name the angle that is vertical to this angle.

_____ _____

2. Chang notices that there appears to be two angle bisectors on the map. Which parts of the map appear to be a bisector?

_____

3. Chang lives at the corner of ∠ACD. Name an angle that is supplementary to ∠ACD.

_____ or _____

Check What You Learned

Problem Solving: Points, Lines, Rays, and Angles

Read the problem carefully and solve. Show your work under each question.

April draws a design. She likes to label points and lines to help plan the design.

---

1. She plans to add line *GH* to her design. Draw the line *GH* below.

2. In the middle of the design, she decided to add the following line segment. How would she name this line segment?

3. April draws two supplementary angles, ∠*F* and ∠*B*. The measure of ∠*F* is 112°. What is the measure of ∠*B*?

_____

4. April draws a right angle as part of her design. She names it ∠*FGH*. Draw and label ∠*FGH* below.

Check What You Know

Geometric Figures

Use the circle to answer the questions.

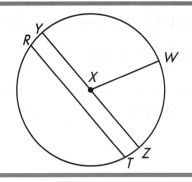

1. Name the circle. _____

2. Name the origin of the circle. _____

3. Name a radius. _____

Identify the triangles as acute (A), obtuse (O), or right (R).

  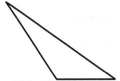 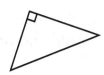

4. _____   _____   _____   _____

Match each term with its picture. You may use a letter more than once. A question may have more than one answer.

5. trapezoid _____

6. triangular pyramid _____

7. rhombus _____

8. cone _____

9. kite _____

10. cylinder _____

11. square _____

12. cube _____

13. rectangle _____

14. triangular solid _____

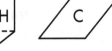

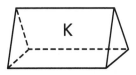

Triangles

A **triangle** is a three-sided figure. The sum of the measures of a triangle is 180°. Triangles are classified by their angles in three categories.

acute triangle	**right triangle**	**obtuse triangle**
Acute angles are greater than 0° and less than 90°.	**Right angles** equal 90°.	**Obtuse angles** are greater than 90°.
	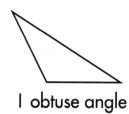 This symbol means right angle.	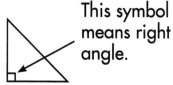
3 acute angles	1 right angle	1 obtuse angle

Identify each triangle below as acute, right, or obtuse.

	a	b	c
1.			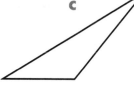
	_____	_____	_____
2.	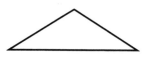		
	_____	_____	_____
3.		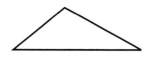	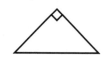
	_____	_____	_____
4.		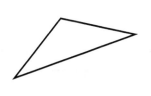	
	_____	_____	_____

Triangles

Identify each triangle below as acute, right, or obtuse.

	a	b	c

1.

_____ _____ _____

2.

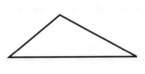

_____ _____ _____

3.

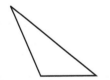 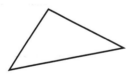

_____ _____ _____

4.

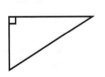  (triangle)

_____ _____ _____

Quadrilaterals

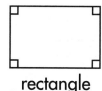 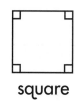 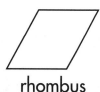 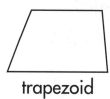 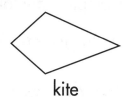

| rectangle | square | rhombus | trapezoid | kite |

A **rectangle** has four right angles, two pairs of parallel sides, and two pairs of congruent sides.

A **square** is a rectangle with four congruent sides.

A **rhombus** has two pairs of parallel sides and four congruent sides.

A **square** is a special kind of rectangle and also a special kind of rhombus.

A **trapezoid** has only one pair of parallel sides.

A **kite** has two pairs of congruent sides but no parallel sides.

Use the figures below to answer each question. Letters may be used more than once. Some questions will have more than one answer. Some letters may not be used.

 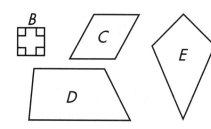 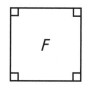 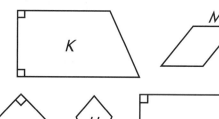

1. Which figure is a rectangle? _____

2. Which figure is a rhombus? _____

3. Which figure is a trapezoid? _____

4. Which figure is a square? _____

5. Which figure is a kite? _____

6. Which figure is a both a rhombus and a rectangle? _____

Quadrilaterals

Complete the following.

1. Which quadrilaterals have four right angles? _____

2. Which quadrilaterals have four congruent sides? _____

3. Are all parallelograms also rectangles? _____

4. Are all rectangles also parallelograms? _____

5. Are all squares also rectangles? _____

6. Are all rectangles also squares? _____

7. Is a square also a rhombus? _____

Identify the following shapes. Use all terms that apply.

a	b

8.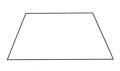

_____ _____

_____ _____

9.

_____ _____

_____ _____

Polygons

A **polygon** is a closed plane figure made up of straight lines. Polygons are named according to the number of their sides. A **triangle** has 3 sides. A **quadrilateral** has 4 sides. A **pentagon** has 5 sides. A **hexagon** has 6 sides.

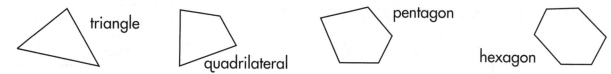

Two polygons are **congruent** if they have exactly the same size and the same shape. Their corresponding sides and their corresponding angles must be congruent. One way to determine if two polygons are congruent is to trace over one of them and match it to the other one. Another way is to measure the corresponding angles and sides.

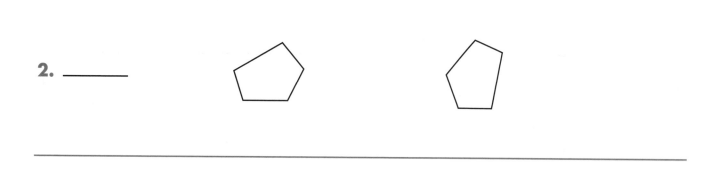

Mark each pair of polygons that are congruent with a C or not congruent with an N.

1. _____

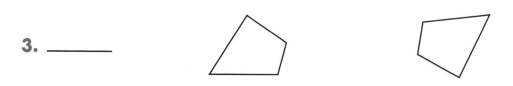

2. _____

3. _____

Polygons

A **polygon** is a closed figure whose sides are all line segments. Polygons can be classified by the number of sides they have. The table shows some of the prefixes of polygons and the number of sides they represent.

Prefix	# of sides
penta-	5
hexa-	6
hepta-	7
octa-	8
nona-	9
deca-	10

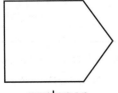

pentagon
5 sides

octagon
8 sides

hexagon
6 sides

Identify the following shapes. Use all terms that apply.

	a	b

1.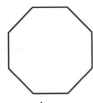

_____ _____

2.

_____ _____

3.

_____ _____

4.

_____ _____

Circles

The **origin** of a circle is a point inside the circle that is the same distance from any point on the circle. A circle is named by its origin.

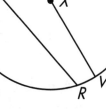

A **radius** of a circle is a line segment with one endpoint at the origin and the other endpoint on the circle.

A **chord** is a line segment with both endpoints on the circle.

A **diameter** is a chord that passes through the origin of the circle.

Name a radius, chord, and diameter of circle X.

radius: $\overline{XZ}$, $\overline{XV}$, or $\overline{XW}$ chord: $\overline{VW}$ or $\overline{SR}$ diameter: $\overline{VW}$

Identify each line segment as radius, chord, or diameter.

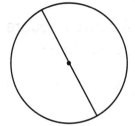 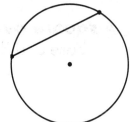  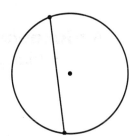

1. _____   _____   _____   _____

Use the figure at the right to answer the questions.

2. Name the circle.   _____

3. Name the origin.   _____

4. Name a radius.   _____

5. Name a chord.   _____

6. Name a diameter.   _____

Solid Figures

A **solid figure** is a three-dimensional figure. A **face** is a flat surface of a solid figure. An **edge** is the intersection of two faces. A **vertex** is a point where three or more faces meet. A **base** is a face on which the solid figure rests.

**A cube has
6 square faces.**

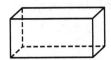

**A rectangular solid
has 6 rectangular faces.**

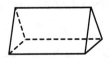

**A triangular solid
has 2 triangular faces
and 3 rectangular faces.**

**A triangular pyramid has
4 triangular faces.**

**A square pyramid has 1 square
base and 4 triangular faces.**

A cone has a circular base and 1 vertex.

A cylinder has 2 circular bases.

Name each figure.

1. A _____

2. B _____

3. C _____

4. D _____

5. E _____

6. F _____

Check What You Learned

Geometric Figures

Use the circle to answer the questions.

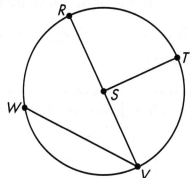

1. Name the circle. _____

2. Name the origin of the circle. _____

3. Name a radius. _____

4. Name a diameter. _____

5. Name a chord that is not a diameter. _____

Complete.

6. Write if the following pairs of polygons are congruent (C) or not congruent (N).

  _____   _____

Match each term with its picture. You may use a letter more than once. A question may have more than one answer.

7. cube _____

8. triangular solid _____

9. triangular pyramid _____

10. rectangular solid _____

11. square pyramid _____

12. trapezoid _____

13. kite _____

14. cylinder _____

15. rhombus _____

16. cone _____

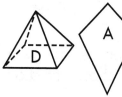

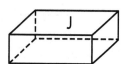 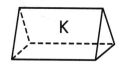

NAME _____

Check What You Know

Problem Solving: Geometric Figures

Read the problem carefully and solve. Show your work under each question.

Carlos and Olivia make a poster. They decorate the poster with different types of shapes.

---

1. Carlos draws an 8-sided figure. What is the name of the polygon?

_____

2. Olivia draws the triangle below. Identify this triangle as acute, right, or obtuse.

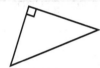

_____

3. Olivia draws the two quadrilaterals shown below. Name the polygons and identify them as congruent or not congruent.

Each polygon is called a _____.

The polygons are _____.

4. Carlos draws a circle. Then, he draws a line segment in the circle. Identify this line segment as a radius, chord, or diameter.

_____

Triangles

Read the problem carefully and solve. Show your work under each question.

Bonnie makes earrings to sell at her jewelry store. She likes to make earrings out of different shapes. This month, she decides to make earrings in the shape of triangles. She plans to use three different types of triangles.

Helpful Hint

Triangles have three sides. The sum of the angle measures in a triangle always equals 180°.

1. **Acute triangles** have three angles that measure less than 90°.

2. **Right triangles** have one right angle. Right angles measure 90°.

3. **Obtuse triangles** have one angle that measures greater than 90°.

---

1. Bonnie makes her first pair of earrings. Each earring is shaped like the triangle below. Identify this triangle as acute, right, or obtuse.

   _____

2. Bonnie makes another pair of earrings. Each earring is shaped like the triangle below. Identify this triangle as acute, right, or obtuse.

   _____

3. Bonnie has a sale on one type of triangular earring. Each earring that is on sale is shaped like the triangle below. Identify this triangle as acute, right, or obtuse.

    _____

Quadrilaterals

Read the problem carefully and solve. Show your work under each question.

Erin is studying quadrilaterals. She learns that small changes in a quadrilateral can give it a new name. She practices the definitions of quadrilaterals by drawing figures on index cards and then writing the definitions on the back of the cards.

1. The definition on the back of one card reads, "a parallelogram with 4 congruent sides." Draw and label two different figures that fit this description.

_____   _____

2. The shape below is on the front of one card. Which two terms will Erin use to name the shape?

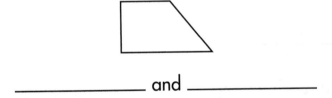

_____ and _____

3. Erin sees the figure shown below on another card as she reviews for a quiz. What terms can be used to name this figure?

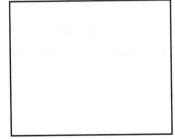

Polygons

Read the problem carefully and solve. Show your work under each question.

Jerry draws different polygons in the sand at the beach. He plays a game where he asks each family member to identify the polygons he draws.

1. Jerry draws a 10-sided figure. What is the name of the polygon?

_____

2. Jerry drew the figure below. What is the name of this figure?

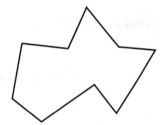

_____

3. Jerry asks his mother to name the figure below that he drew in the sand. What is the name of the figure?

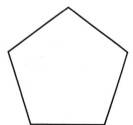

_____

SCORE ⬭ / 2

Circles

Read the problem carefully and solve. Show your work under each question.

Carolyn designs sets of circular coasters. First, she draws a diagram of her design in pencil. Then, she labels her drawing using letters. The circle to the right shows Carolyn's design.

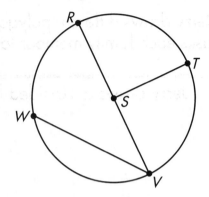

Helpful Hint

The **origin** of a circle is the center point inside the circle. A circle is named by its origin.

A **radius** of a circle is a line segment with one endpoint at the origin and the other endpoint on the circle.

A **chord** is a line segment with both endpoints on the circle.

A **diameter** is a chord that passes through the origin of the circle.

1. Name the origin of the circle.

   _____

2. Carolyn starts another circle design for a new set of coasters. She draws a line segment in the circle below. Identify this line segment as a radius, chord, or diameter.

   _____

Circles

3. Name a diameter in Carolyn's circle design. If there is more than one, list them all.

_____

4. Name a radius in the circle. If there is more than one, list them all.

_____

5. Name a chord in Carolyn's circle that is not a diameter.

_____

Solid Figures

Read the problem carefully and solve. Show your work under each question.

Masako plans to use the solid figures below in a model that he will build for a school project. Before he starts, he decides to keep track of the number of **faces**, **vertices**, and **edges** for each solid.

triangular pyramid

cone

triangular solid

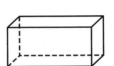
rectangular solid

square pyramid

cylinder

> **Helpful Hint**
>
> A **face** is a flat surface of a solid figure.
>
> An **edge** is the intersection of two faces.
>
> A **vertex** is a point where three or more faces meet.
>
> A **base** is a face on which a solid figure rests.

1. Which of Masako's solids has the largest number of vertices? How many does it have?

2. Masako notices that two of the solids have the same number of faces. What are these two solids?

Solid Figures

3. How many more edges does a square pyramid have than a triangular pyramid?

_____

4. One of Masako's solids has no vertices. Which one is it?

_____

5. The first shape Masako is going to use in his model has only one vertex and a circular base. What is the name of this solid?

_____

Quadrilaterals and Polygons

Read the problem carefully and solve. Show your work under each question.

Joanne and Natalia make a quilt with seven different types of polygons cut out of cloth. Before they start, they sort the polygons below in a variety of ways. They give each type of polygon a letter to make the sorting easier.

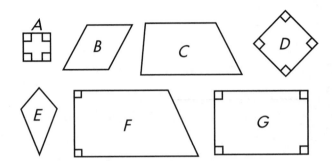

1. Natalia sorts all the polygons to find the ones that are rectangles. Write the letters of the polygons that are rectangles.

_____

2. Natalia cuts out the two polygons below from purple cloth. Name the polygons and identify them as congruent or not congruent.

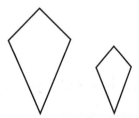

Each polygon is called a _____.

The polygons are _____.

3. Joanne cuts out the two polygons below from red cloth. Identify the polygons as congruent or not congruent.

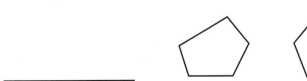

_____

Check What You Learned

Problem Solving: Geometric Figures

Read the problem carefully and solve. Show your work under each question.

Masako builds a model for his school project. He decides to use polygons and circles as well as solid figures in his model.

I. Masako's model has nine sides. What is the name of the polygon?

_____

2. Masako draws the triangle below. Identify this triangle as acute, right, or obtuse.

_____

3. Masako draws a polygon with seven sides. What is the name of this polygon?

_____

4. Masako draws a line segment in the circle. Identify this line segment as a radius, chord, or diameter in the circle below.

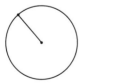

_____

Draw and name the following figures.

1. line *CD*   •*C*   •*D*   _____

   line segment *DC*   •*C*   •*D*   _____

Name each figure.

2.

_____   _____   _____

Use the circle to answer the questions.

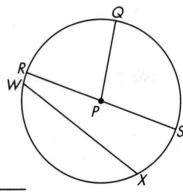

3. Name the circle.   _____

4. The origin of the circle is   _____ .

5. A radius of the circle is   _____ .

6. A diameter of the circle is   _____ .

7. Specify a chord that is not a diameter. _____

Answer the questions about the angles below. ∠*m* = 55°, ∠*x* = 35°

8. ∠*Y* = _____

9. ∠*Z* = _____

10. ∠*W* = _____

11. ∠*N* = _____

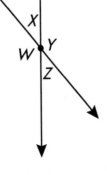

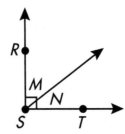

Mid-Test Chapters 1–4

Read the problem carefully and solve. Show your work under each question.

Jamal makes a design for a new park. The park will have a bricked area with picnic tables, gardens, and walking paths. He draws and labels a blueprint of the picnic area on a coordinate grid for the construction workers. He also draws a map of the park showing the gardens and the walking paths.

12. Jamal wants to cover part of the picnic area with a roof. The roof is shaped like the solid figure below. How many faces does it have?

 _____ faces

13. Jamal adds a circular garden to the map of the park. He will plant bushes on part of the garden and flowers on the other part. He draws a line segment in the circle below to show the two sides of the garden. Identify this line segment as a radius, chord, or diameter.

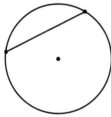 _____

14. Jamal draws straight lines on the map to represent two walking paths that intersect. This intersection forms two supplementary angles. He labels these two supplementary angles, $\angle L$ and $\angle M$. The measure of $\angle L$ is 138°. What is the measure of $\angle M$?

_____

15. Jamal draws another garden in the shape of the triangle shown below. Identify this triangle as acute, right, or obtuse.

 _____

NAME _____

Check What You Know

Perimeter, Area, and Volume

Find the perimeter of each figure.

1.

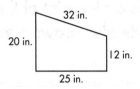

32 in.

20 in.

12 in.

25 in.

perimeter = _____ inches

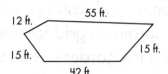

12 ft.   55 ft.

15 ft.   15 ft.

42 ft.

perimeter = _____ feet

Find the area of each right triangle.

2.

15 in.

42 in.

area = _____ square inches

17 ft.

9 ft.

area = _____ square feet

Find the volume of each rectangular solid.

3.

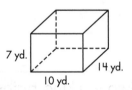

7 yd.

14 yd.

10 yd.

volume = _____ cubic yards

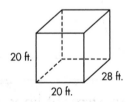

20 ft.

28 ft.

20 ft.

volume = _____ cubic feet

Find the surface area of each figure.

4.

12 in.

10 in.

13 in.

_____ sq. in.

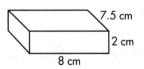

7.5 cm

2 cm

8 cm

_____ sq. cm

Measuring Perimeter

The **perimeter** is the distance around a figure. To find the perimeter, find the sum of the lengths of its sides.

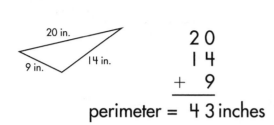

$$\begin{array}{r} 20 \\ 14 \\ + \ 9 \\ \hline \end{array}$$

perimeter = 43 inches

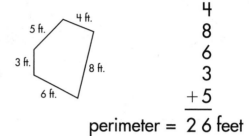

$$\begin{array}{r} 4 \\ 8 \\ 6 \\ 3 \\ + 5 \\ \hline \end{array}$$

perimeter = 26 feet

Find the perimeter of each figure.

a

b

1.

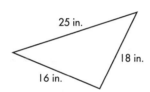

perimeter = _____ inches

perimeter = _____ feet

2.

perimeter = _____ yards

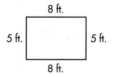

perimeter = _____ feet

Perimeter

Find the perimeter of each figure.

a	b	c

1.

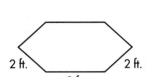

2 ft.   2 ft.
3 ft.

_____ ft.

4 yd.
5 yd.
4 yd.

_____ yd.

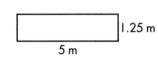

1.25 m
5 m

_____ m

2.

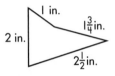

1 in.
$1\frac{3}{4}$ in.
2 in.
$2\frac{1}{2}$ in.

_____ in.

16 cm

_____ cm

9 yd.   9 yd.
9 yd.

_____ yd.

3.

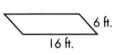

6 ft.
16 ft.

_____ ft.

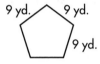

3.1 m   3.1 m
2.8 m

_____ m

2 in.
3 in.

_____ in.

4.

3 m

_____ m

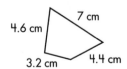

7 cm
4.6 cm
3.2 cm   4.4 cm

_____ cm

26 yd.
14 yd.

_____ yd.

SCORE ⬭ /9

Area of Rectangles

Area is the number of square units it takes to cover a figure. To find the area of a rectangle, multiply the length by the width.

 length 7 units, width 2 units

$A = 7 \times 2$
$A = 14$ square units

8 units

$A = s \times s = 8 \times 8$
$A = 64$ square units

Find the area of each rectangle below.

	a	**b**	**c**

1.

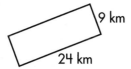 3 yd. / 6 yd.

18 m

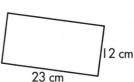 12 cm / 23 cm

_____ square yards   _____ square meters   _____ square centimeters

2.

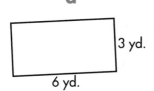 9 km / 24 km

23 in.

 8 ft. / 6 ft.

_____ square kilometers   _____ square inches   _____ square feet

---

Find the missing length of each rectangle below.

3.

 6 in.

4.5 ft.

 9 m

$A = 54$ sq. in. $A = 58.5$ sq. ft. $A = 81$ sq. m

$l =$ _____ in. $l =$ _____ ft. $l =$ _____ m

Area of Right Triangles

The **area** (A) of a right triangle is one-half the product of the measure of its base (b) and the measure of its height (h). $A = \frac{1}{2} \times b \times h$

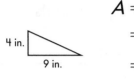

$A = \frac{1}{2} \times 9 \times 4$
$\quad = \frac{1}{2} \times 36$
$\quad = 18$
$A = 18$ square inches

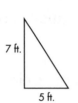

$A = \frac{1}{2} \times 5 \times 7$
$\quad = \frac{1}{2} \times 35$
$\quad = 17\frac{1}{2}$
$A = 17\frac{1}{2}$ square feet

Find the area of each right triangle.

a **b**

1.

10 in.

8 in.

area = _____ square inches

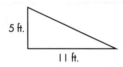

5 ft.

11 ft.

area = _____ square feet

2.

5 ft.

5 ft.

area = _____ square feet

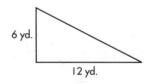

6 yd.

12 yd.

area = _____ square yards

Area of Triangles

Find the area of each right triangle.

         a   **b**   **c**

1.

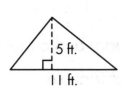   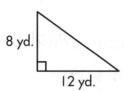   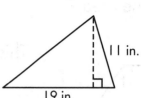

_____ sq. ft.   _____ sq. yd.   _____ sq. in.

2.

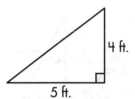   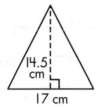   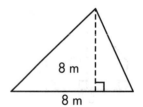

_____ sq. ft.   _____ sq. cm   _____ sq. m

3.

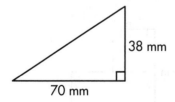   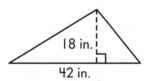   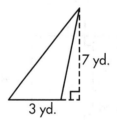

_____ sq. mm   _____ sq. in.   _____ sq. yd.

Area of Irregular Shapes

To find the area of irregular shapes, separate the shapes into figures for which you can find the area.

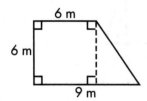

6 m
6 m
9 m

This figure can be divided into a square and a triangle.

area of square

$A = 6 \times 6 = 36$

area of triangle

$A = \frac{1}{2} \times 3 \times 6 = 9$

The area of the figure is $36 + 9 = 45$ square meters.

Find the area of each figure.

a	b	c

1.

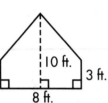

10 ft.
3 ft.
8 ft.

____ square feet

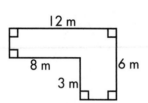

12 m
8 m
6 m
3 m

____ square meters

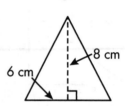

8 cm
6 cm

____ square centimeters

2.

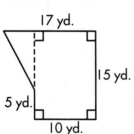

17 yd.
15 yd.
5 yd.
10 yd.

____ square yards

4 mi.
3 mi.
2 mi.

____ square miles

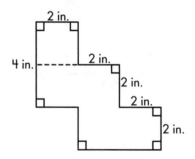

2 in.
4 in.
2 in.
2 in.
2 in.
2 in.

____ square inches

SCORE ⬭/4

Area of Irregular Shapes

Find the area of each figure.

a

b

1.

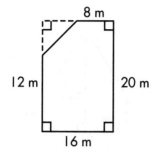

A = _____ m²

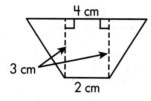

A = _____ cm²

2.

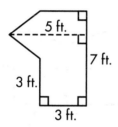

A = _____ ft.²

A = _____ in.²

SCORE  / 4

Area of Irregular Shapes

Find the area of each figure.

a b

1.

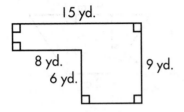

A = _____ yd.²

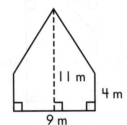

A = _____ m²

2.

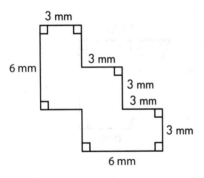

A = _____ mm²

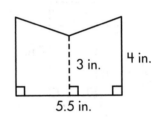

A = _____ in.²

Surface Area of a Rectangular Solid

The **surface area** of a solid is the sum of the areas of all the faces (or surfaces) of the solid. A rectangular solid has six surfaces.

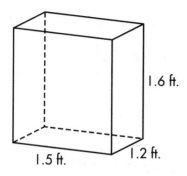

The area of each surface is determined by finding length × width, length × height, and width × height. Calculate the total surface area using the formula $SA = 2lw + 2lh + 2wh$.

In the figure on the left, $l = 1.5$ ft., $w = 1.2$ ft., and $h = 1.6$ ft.

$SA = 2(1.5 \text{ ft.})(1.2 \text{ ft.}) + 2(1.5 \text{ ft.})(1.6 \text{ ft.}) + 2(1.2 \text{ ft.})(1.6 \text{ ft.})$

$SA = 3.6 \text{ ft.}^2 + 4.8 \text{ ft.}^2 + 3.82 \text{ ft}^2$

$SA = 12.22 \text{ ft.}^2$

Find the surface area of each figure.

        a   **b**

1.

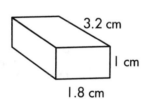

$SA = $ _____ cm^2

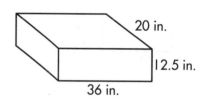

$SA = $ _____ $in.^2$

2.

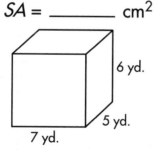

$SA = $ _____ $yd.^2$

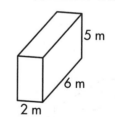

$SA = $ _____ m^2

3.

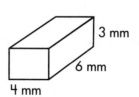

$SA = $ _____ mm^2

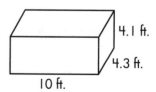

$SA = $ _____ $ft.^2$

SCORE ⬤ /9

Surface Area of a Rectangular Solid

Find the surface area of each figure.

a	b	c

1.

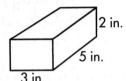

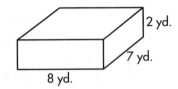

_____ square inches _____ square feet _____ square yards

2.

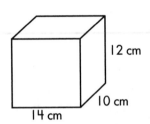

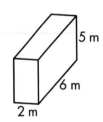

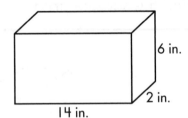

_____ square centimeters _____ square meters _____ square inches

3.

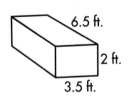

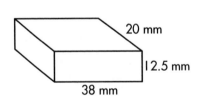

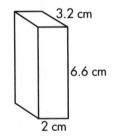

_____ square feet _____ square millimeters _____ square centimeters

Measuring Volume

The **volume** (*V*) measure of a rectangular solid is the product of the measure of its length (*l*), the measure of its width (*w*), and the measure of its height (*h*).
$V = l \times w \times h$

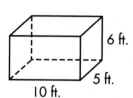

6 ft.
5 ft.
10 ft.

$V = 10 \times 5 \times 6$
$= 50 \times 6$
$= 300$
The volume is 300 cubic feet.

Find the volume of each figure.

a

b

1.

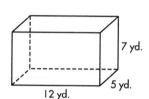

7 yd.
5 yd.
12 yd.

volume = _____ cubic yards

8 in.
8 in.
8 in.

volume = _____ cubic inches

2.

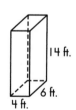

14 ft.
6 ft.
4 ft.

volume = _____ cubic feet

5 in.
5 in.
4 in.

volume = _____ cubic inches

3.

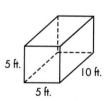

5 ft.
10 ft.
5 ft.

volume = _____ cubic feet

5 in.
15 in.
4 in.

volume = _____ cubic inches

Volume of Rectangular Solids

The **volume** of a rectangular solid is the product of the length times width times height. The product of the length times width is the base. The formula for the volume is $V = B \times h$. Volume is expressed in cubic units.

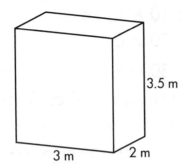

$B = 3 \times 2 = 6$

$V = B \times h = 6 \times 3.5$

$V = 21$ cubic meters

Find the volume of each figure.

	a	**b**	**c**

1.

_____ cubic feet   _____ cubic meters   _____ cubic inches

2.

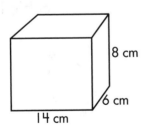
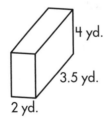
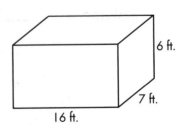

_____ cubic centimeters   _____ cubic yards   _____ cubic feet

Volume of Rectangular Prism

Find the volume of each figure.

a b

1.

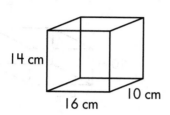

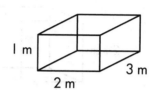

_____ cm³   _____ m³

2.

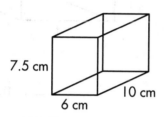

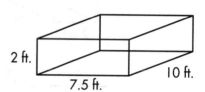

_____ cm³   _____ ft.³

3.

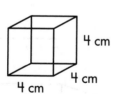

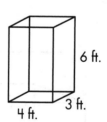

_____ cm³   _____ ft.³

SCORE ◯ / 8

Volume of Rectangular Prism

Find the volume of each figure.

a	b

1.

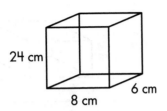

24 cm   6 cm   8 cm

_____ cm³

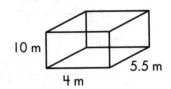

10 m   5.5 m   4 m

_____ m³

2.

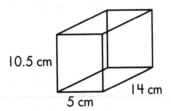

10.5 cm   14 cm   5 cm

_____ cm³

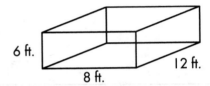

6 ft.   12 ft.   8 ft.

_____ ft.³

3.

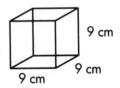

9 cm   9 cm   9 cm

_____ cm³

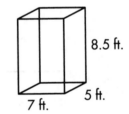

8.5 ft.   7 ft.   5 ft.

_____ ft.³

4.

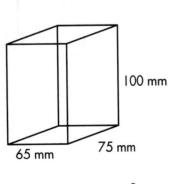

100 mm   75 mm   65 mm

_____ mm³

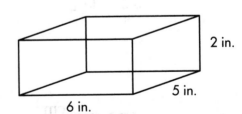

2 in.   5 in.   6 in.

_____ in.³

Check What You Learned

Perimeter and Area

Find the perimeter of each figure.

a	b	c

1.

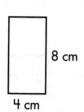 8 cm, 4 cm

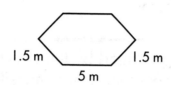 1.5 m, 1.5 m, 5 m

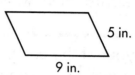 5 in., 9 in.

$P =$ _____ cm $P =$ _____ m $P =$ _____ in.

Find the unknown measure, area, or perimeter.

2.

  $A = 196 \text{ m}^2$

  5.5 yd., 7.5 yd.

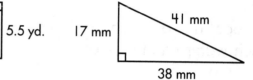 41 mm, 17 mm, 38 mm

$s =$ _____ m $A =$ _____ yd.^{2} $A =$ _____ mm^2

$P =$ _____ m $P =$ _____ yd. $P =$ _____ mm

Find the area for the parallelograms and irregular shapes.

3.

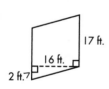 17 ft., 16 ft., 2 ft.7

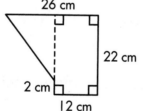 26 cm, 22 cm, 2 cm, 12 cm

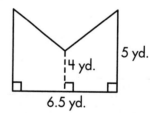 5 yd., 4 yd., 6.5 yd.

$A =$ _____ ft.^{2} $A =$ _____ cm^2 $A =$ _____ yd.^{2}

Find the volume of each rectangular prism.

4.

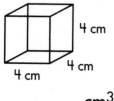 4 cm, 4 cm, 4 cm

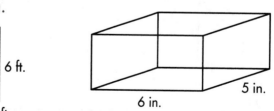 6 ft., 3 ft., 4 ft., 2 in., 5 in., 6 in.

_____ cm^3 _____ ft.^{3} _____ in.^{3}

CHAPTER 5 POSTTEST

Check What You Know

Problem Solving: Perimeter, Area, and Volume

Read the problem carefully and solve. Show your work under each question.

Greg spends a week over the summer at an overnight camp. He records many things about his environment while at camp.

1. The layout of the camp is represented by the drawing shown below. There is a fence around the property. How long is the fence?

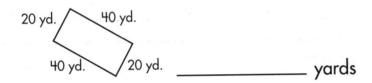

_____ yards

2. The pool has a length of 12 feet, width of 8 feet, and a depth of 5 feet. How much water can the pool hold?

_____ cubic feet

3. Greg makes a clay slate in one of his activities at camp. The picture below shows the slate. What is the area of the slate?

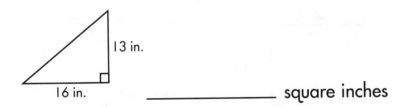

_____ square inches

4. Greg makes the following object while at camp and wants to paint its sides. What is the surface area of the object?

_____ square inches

Perimeter

Read the problem carefully and solve. Show your work under each question.

Joanna works for a fencing company. Her job is to determine the amount of fencing needed for various clients.

Helpful Hint

The **perimeter** of a figure is the sum of the lengths of its sides. If two or more sides are equal, the formula can be simplified with multiplication.

I. Joanna needs to determine the perimeter of an animal pen. How many yards is the perimeter of the pen?

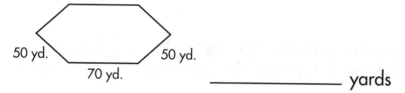

50 yd.   50 yd.
70 yd.   _____ yards

2. The figure below represents a city park in the shape of a regular pentagon. The city puts a fence around the park. How many yards of fencing is needed?

30 yd.   30 yd.
              30 yd.   _____ yards

3. A parking lot is represented by the rectangle below. Joanna's company is hired to put a fence around the lot. How many yards of fencing will be needed?

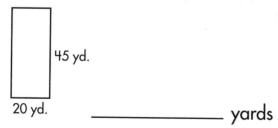

45 yd.

20 yd.   _____ yards

Area of Rectangles

Read the problem carefully and solve. Show your work under each question.

Ivan sells rugs that are either square or rectangular in shape. He prices the rugs based on their square footage.

1. Ivan sells the rug below to a new customer. What is the area of this rug?

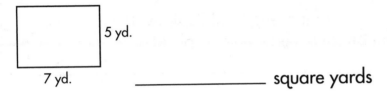

_____ square yards

2. The most popular rug that Ivan sells is represented by the figure below. A customer at the store wants to know the area of this rug. Write the area below.

_____ square feet

3. On Saturday, Ivan sells a large rug to a restaurant. The rug measures 24 feet by 18 feet. What is the area of the rug?

_____ square feet

SCORE ⬤ /3

Area of Triangles

Read the problem carefully and solve. Show your work under each question.

Hugo makes ceramic tiles that are triangular in shape. He sells his tiles to friends and businesses in the town where he lives.

---

1. One type of tile Hugo makes that is often purchased for kitchen counters is shown below. Find the area of the tile.

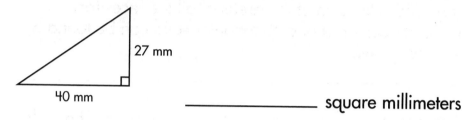

_____ square millimeters

2. Hugo makes tiles for his mother in the shape shown below. She plans to use them in her living room. What is the area of each tile?

_____ square centimeters

3. Hugo makes a pattern using only tiles like the one shown below. He wants to know how many tiles can fit on the counter where he is building out the pattern. Find the area of each tile.

_____ square inches

SCORE ◯ **/2**

Surface Area

Read the problem carefully and solve. Show your work under each question.

Mr. Benson sells packaging boxes. The boxes come in a variety of sizes.

> **Helpful Hint**
>
> The **surface area** of a solid is the sum of the areas of all the faces (or surfaces of the solid). The surface area of a rectangular solid can be found by the formula $SA = 2lw + 2lh + 2wh$.

1. The picture below represents the building that Mr. Benson works in. The surface area of the building is 416 square yards. What is the height of the building?

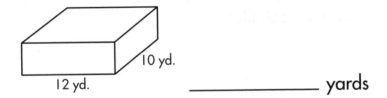

12 yd.   10 yd.

_____ yards

2. Mr. Benson buys a jewelry box for his daughter. The box measures 7 inches by 5 inches by 3 inches. What is the surface area of the box?

_____ square inches

Surface Area

1. The most popular-sized box Mr. Benson sells has the dimensions of 32 cm by 12 cm by 26 cm. What is the surface area of this box?

_____ square centimeters

2. Mr. Benson has a customer who wants to know the surface area of the box below so she can buy enough gift-wrap for the box. What is the surface area of the box?

_____ square inches

3. One of Mr. Benson's customers buys the box below to send some books through the mail. What is the surface area of the box?

_____ square inches

SCORE ◯ **/3**

Area of Irregular Shapes

Read the problem carefully and solve. Show your work under each question.

Olivia learns about irregular shapes in school. Then, she begins to notice all sorts of irregular shapes in the world around her.

1. Olivia looks at a drawing of her parents' property and then draws the shape below to represent it. What is the area of the property?

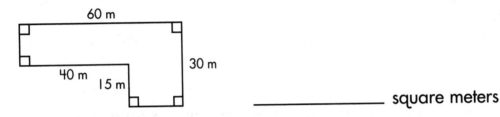

_____ square meters

2. Olivia's family has a cottage by a lake. The picture below shows the layout of the cottage. What is the area?

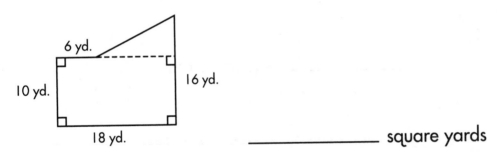

_____ square yards

3. Olivia finds a plastic shape in her house that has the dimensions shown below. What is the area of the shape?

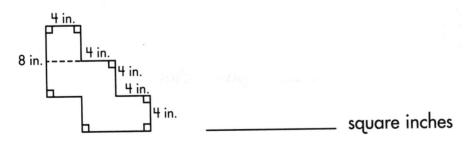

_____ square inches

Volume of Rectangular Solids

Read the problem carefully and solve. Show your work under each question.

Daysha works on a container ship that carries cargo. Daysha records the volume of each container that is loaded onto the ship.

1. One of the containers on the ship contains cameras. The dimensions of this container are shown below. Find the volume of the container.

_____ cubic centimeters

2. The container shown below is filled with office supplies and loaded onto the ship by Daysha. The volume of the container is 225 cubic feet. What is the width?

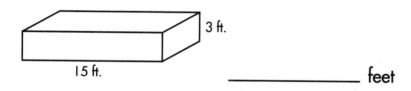

_____ feet

3. Daysha loads a container onto the ship that is packed with furniture. The drawing below shows the dimensions of this container. What is its volume?

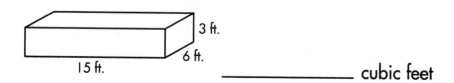

_____ cubic feet

Measuring Perimeter, Area, and Volume

Read the problem carefully and solve. Show your work under each question.

Don builds a jewelry box for his mother. He wants the jewelry box to have a length of 20 centimeters, a width of 8 centimeters, and a height of 8 centimeters. To build this, Don will need 6 pieces of wood: 2 pieces shaped like squares, and 4 pieces shaped like rectangles.

1. The 2 square-shaped pieces of wood Don uses are the same size. One of the squares is shown below. What is the perimeter of the square?

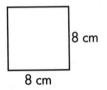
8 cm

8 cm

_____ cm

2. What is the area of each square-shaped piece of wood that Don uses?

_____ sq. cm

3. The rectangular solid below shows the dimensions of the jewelry box when it is completed. What is the volume of the box?

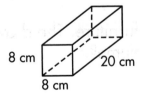
8 cm   20 cm
8 cm

_____ cu. cm

Measuring Perimeter, Area, and Volume

Read the problem carefully and solve. Show your work under each question.

Mr. Adams had his students cut shapes out of construction paper for a game he wants to play with his class. In this game, students choose shapes out of a box. He had his students cut out triangles and 4-sided shapes.

1. Ron cut out the rectangle below. What is the perimeter of the rectangle?

_____ in.

2. Melissa cut out the trapezoid below. What is the perimeter of the trapezoid?

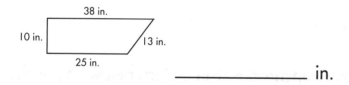

_____ in.

3. Carlos cut out the right triangle below. What is the area of the triangle?

_____ sq. in.

NAME _____

 Check What You Learned

Problem Solving: Perimeter, Area, and Volume

Read the problem carefully and solve. Show your work under each question.

Delia works in the maintenance department for a local business.

1. Delia has an office space, shown below, that is in the shape of a square. She needs to run an electric cord around the edge of the space. How long will the cord be?

6 ft.

_____ feet

2. The diagram below represents Delia's office building. The maintenance crew needs to calculate the total volume of the building for the new air-conditioning system. What is the volume of the building?

45 ft.

32 ft.

44 ft.

_____ cubic feet

3. The company that Delia works for has a lunchroom. The picture below shows the room. What is its area?

20 ft.

16 ft.

_____ square feet

4. Delia has a bin to store her paper clips in. What are the surface area and volume of the bin?

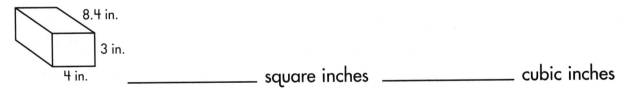

8.4 in.

3 in.

4 in.

_____ square inches _____ cubic inches

Check What You Know

The Coordinate Plane

Add or subtract the following integers.

	a	b	c
1.	$2 - 18 = $ _____	$-7 - (-7) = $ _____	$-15 + (-6) = $ _____
2.	$-3 - (-9) = $ _____	$2 + 3 = $ _____	$7 - 18 = $ _____
3.	$10 + 4 = $ _____	$-17 + (-3) = $ _____	$-5 + 14 = $ _____
4.	$12 + (-5) = $ _____	$4 - 9 = $ _____	$-2 + 2 = $ _____

Use the grid to name a point for each ordered pair.

5. $(8, 4)$ _____ $(7, 2)$ _____

6. $(9, 1)$ _____ $(9, 9)$ _____

Use the same grid, name the ordered pair
for each point.

7. $C ($ _____ , _____ $)$ $A ($ _____ , _____ $)$

8. $F ($ _____ , _____ $)$ $H ($ _____ , _____ $)$

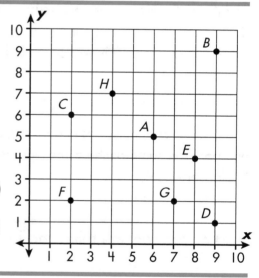

Plot the points shown on the grid. Label the points.

9. $M (4, 4)$ $N (-6, -6)$

10. $O (-4, 6)$ $P (5, -4)$

11. $Q (-3, -3)$ $R (9, 2)$

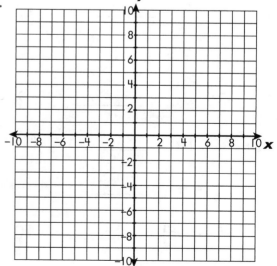

SCORE ⬭ **/ 18**

Working with Integers

Integers are the set of whole numbers and their opposites. **Positive integers** are greater than zero. **Negative integers** are less than zero, and they are always less than positive integers.

The sum of two positive integers is a positive integer. $4 + 3 = 7$

The sum of two negative integers is a negative integer. $-4 + (-3) = -7$

To find the sum of a positive and negative integer, first find their absolute values. **Absolute value** is the distance (in units) that a number is from 0 expressed as a positive quantity. It is written as $|x|$.

To add -4 and 3, find the absolute values.

$|-4| = 4$

$|3| = 3$

$4 - 3 = -1$

Then, subtract the lesser number from the greater number. The sum has the same sign as the integer with the larger absolute value.

Since 4 is negative, the answer is negative.

$5 - 7 = 5 + (-7) = -2$

Add or subtract the following integers.

	a	b	c
1.	$6 + 3 =$ _____	$10 + (-2) =$ _____	$-5 + 13 =$ _____
2.	$2 - 9 =$ _____	$-3 - 6 =$ _____	$7 - (-5) =$ _____
3.	$-35 - 0 =$ _____	$-2 + (-7) =$ _____	$-13 + (-7) =$ _____
4.	$7 - 19 =$ _____	$11 + (-33) =$ _____	$12 - 23 =$ _____
5.	$-4 + 4 =$ _____	$-1 + 3 =$ _____	$9 + (-8) =$ _____
6.	$-5 + (-5) =$ _____	$10 - (-1) =$ _____	$-13 - 6 =$ _____

Plotting Ordered Pairs

The position of any point on a grid can be described by an **ordered pair** of numbers. The two numbers are named in order: (x, y). Point A on the grid at the right is named by the ordered pair (3, 2). It is located at 3 on the horizontal scale (x) and 2 on the vertical scale (y). The number on the horizontal scale is always named first in an ordered pair. Point B is named by the ordered pair (7, 3).

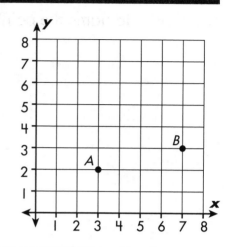

Use Grid 1 to name the point or ordered pair.

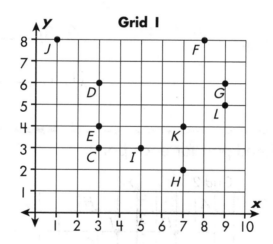

1.   (7, 2) _____   (3, 4) _____

2.   (3, 6) _____   (9, 6) _____

3.   L (_____, _____)   C (_____, _____)

4.   J (_____, _____)   I (_____, _____)

5.   F (_____, _____)   K (_____, _____)

Plotting Ordered Pairs

Use Grid 1 to name the point for each ordered pair.

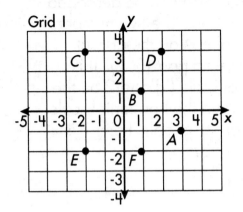

	a		**b**	
1.	(2, 3) _____		(3, -1) _____	
2.	(-2, -2) _____		(-2, 3) _____	
3.	(1, -2) _____		(1, 1) _____	

Use Grid 2 to find the ordered pair for each point.

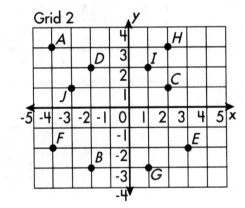

	a	**b**
4.	A (_____ , _____)	F (_____ , _____)
5.	B (_____ , _____)	G (_____ , _____)
6.	C (_____ , _____)	H (_____ , _____)

Drawing Shapes

A polygon is a closed shape created by straight lines. The vertices of a polygon are the points where the lines intersect. These vertices can be described by coordinates and plotted on a coordinate plane. When the points are connected by straight lines, they form a polygon.

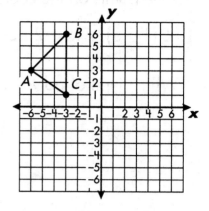

The points A(−6, 3), B(−3, 6), and C(−3, 1) are plotted on a coordinate plane. When the points are connected with straight lines, they form a triangle, a type of polygon.

Plot the points on the coordinate plane and connect the points with straight lines.

1. A(−2, 3), B(2, 3), C(−4, −2), D(4, −2)

   Which type of polygon did you draw?

   _____

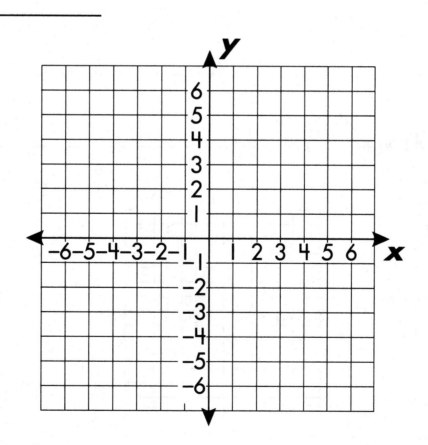

Drawing Shapes

Plot the points on the coordinate plane and connect the points with straight lines.

1. $E(1, -3)$, $F(5, -2)$, $G(5, -5)$, $H(4, -3)$

Which type of polygon did you draw?_____

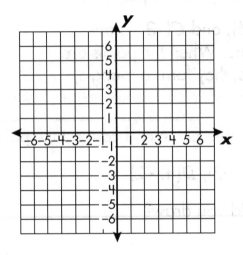

2. $I(-3, 5)$, $J(4, 5)$, $K(1, 2)$, $L(-6, 2)$

Which type of polygon did you draw?_____

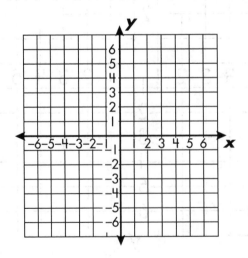

SCORE ◯ **/ 3**

Plotting Ordered Pairs

Read the problem carefully and solve. Show your work under each question.

Irene draws a coordinate plane and plots points to help her decide where to paint flowers on her bedroom wall. The grid is shown to the right.

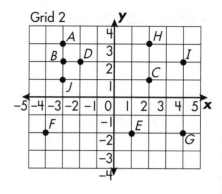

1. Irene plans to paint a lilac flower at point (4, 2) on the grid. Which letter represents this point?

   _____

2. If Irene moves point *H* two units to the right, what will be the coordinate location of the new point on the grid?

   _____

3. Irene plans to paint a rose at point (−3, 3) on the grid. Which letter represents this point?

   _____

Check What You Learned

The Coordinate Plane

Add or subtract the following integers.

	a	b	c
1.	$5 + 9 =$ _____	$12 - 15 =$ _____	$-6 + (-20) =$ _____
2.	$17 - 23 =$ _____	$-8 - (-4) =$ _____	$7 - 18 =$ _____
3.	$13 + 2 =$ _____	$11 - (-6) =$ _____	$-3 + (-6) =$ _____
4.	$-5 + 1 =$ _____	$32 - (-9) =$ _____	$6 - 4 =$ _____

Use the grid to name a point for each ordered pair.

5. (8, 7) _____   (4, 3) _____

6. (1, 7) _____   (3, 5) _____

Using the same grid, name the ordered pair
for each point.

7. A (_____ , _____)   H (_____ , _____)

8. F (_____ , _____)   D (_____ , _____)

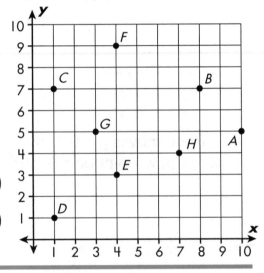

Plot the points shown on the grid. Label the points.

9. M (-3, -4)   N (9, -6)

10. O (-5, 7)   P (7, -2)

11. Q (-7, 2)   R (8, 7)

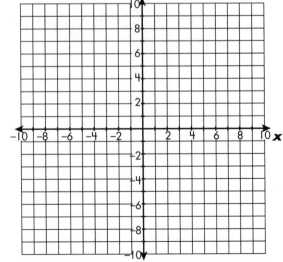

Final Test Chapters 1–7

Identify each of the following and name it.

1. A •——→ B _____ _____   R •—— S _____ _____

2. ←•——→ C   D _____ _____   ←•——•→ J   K _____ _____

3. ←•——• E   F _____ _____   •——• L   M _____ _____

Name the angles and tell if they are acute (A), obtuse (O), or right (R).

4.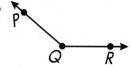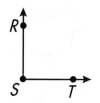

_____   _____   _____

Identify each pair of angles as vertical (V), supplementary (S), or complementary (C).

5. ∠A and ∠C = _____

6. ∠A and ∠B = _____

7. ∠B and ∠D = _____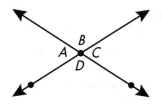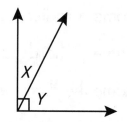

8. ∠B and ∠C = _____

9. ∠X and ∠Y = _____

Identify the triangles as acute (A), obtuse (O), or right (R).

10. 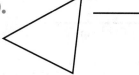 _____   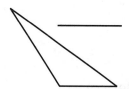 _____   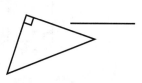 _____   _____

Final Test Chapters 1–7

Add or subtract the following integers.

<table>
<tr><td>a</td><td>b</td><td>c</td></tr>
</table>

11. 7 + 11 = _____   2 – 1 = _____   7 – 18 = _____

Plot the following coordinates on the grid and connect the points by straight lines.

12. A (3, 3), B (6, 6), C (10, 6), D (7, 3)

E (3, –3), F (7, –3), G (10, –6), H (6, –6)

13. What type of polygon did you draw?

_____

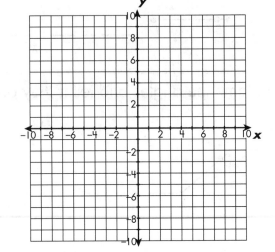

Use the figure at the right to answer the questions.

14. Name the circle. _____

15. Name the origin. _____

16. Name a radius. _____

17. Name a chord. _____

18. Name the diameter. _____

Find the area of each figure.

19.

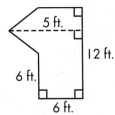

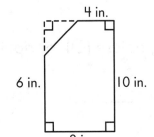

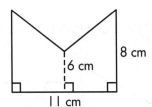

_____ square feet   _____ square inches   _____ square centimeters

Final Test Chapters 1–7

Find the volume of each figure.

a

b

20.

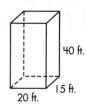

40 ft.

15 ft.

20 ft.

volume = _____ cubic feet

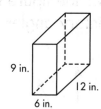

9 in.

12 in.

6 in.

volume = _____ cubic inches

Find the surface area of each figure.

21.

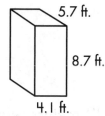

5.7 ft.

8.7 ft.

4.1 ft.

SA = _____ ft.^{2}

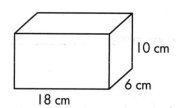

10 cm

6 cm

18 cm

SA = _____ cm^2

Plot the points on the coordinate plane and connect the points with straight lines.

22. $E(1, -3)$, $F(5, -1)$, $G(5, -5)$, $H(4, -3)$

23. Which type of polygon did you draw?

_____

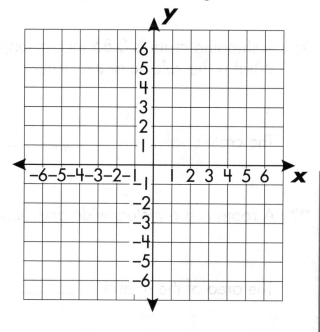

Final Test Chapters 1–7

Solve each problem.

24. Jayden draws the figure below. Identify ∠X and ∠Y as complementary, vertical, or supplementary angles. Solve for the measure of ∠X if ∠Y = 38°.

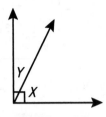

∠X and ∠Y are _____ angles.

∠X measures _____.

25. Craig's backyard is a rectangle 25 meters long and 20 meters wide. What is the perimeter of Craig's yard?

The perimeter of Craig's yard is _____ meters.

26. A shipping crate is 0.85 meters long, 0.4 meters wide, and 0.3 meters high. What is the volume of the crate?

The crate's volume is _____ cubic meters.

27. A room is 8.6 meters wide and 10.2 meters long. What is the area of the room?

The area of the room is _____ square meters.

Final Test Chapters 1–7

Solve each problem. Show your work.

28. Mr. Ruiz wants to put a fence around his backyard. The yard is a rectangle 50 feet long and 28 feet wide. How many feet of fence will he need?

Mr. Ruiz will need _____ feet of fence.

29. Andrew has an aquarium that is 16 inches long, 10 inches wide, and 9 inches deep. What is the volume of Andrew's aquarium?

The volume of Andrew's aquarium is _____ cubic inches.

30. A city park is shaped like a right triangle. Its base is 20 yards and its depth is 48 yards. What is the area of the park?

The area of the park is _____ square yards.

The third side of the park is 52 yards. What is the perimeter of the park?

The perimeter is _____ yards.

31. A paving brick is 3 inches wide, 2 inches high, and 6 inches long. What is the volume of the brick?

The volume is _____ cubic inches.

Final Test Chapters 1–7

Solve each problem. Show your work.

31. A drawing of a house is made up of a rectangle for the walls and a triangle for the roof. The base of the drawing is 9 inches wide. The height of the walls is 7 inches. And the height to the top of the roof is 10 inches. What is the area of the house in the drawing?

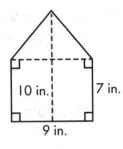

10 in. 7 in.

9 in.

The area of the drawing is _____ square inches.

32. A building with a flat roof is 11 meters long, 8 meters wide, and 6 meters high. What is the surface area?

The surface area of the building is _____ square meters.

33. An aquarium is 50 centimeters long, 20 centimeters wide, and 30 centimeters high. How many cubic centimeters of water can it hold?

The aquarium can hold _____ cubic centimeters of water.

34. Opal needs to wrap a box. The box is 12 inches by 8 inches by 1.5 inches. If she wants to wrap it with no overlap, how much paper does she need?

Opal needs _____ square inches of paper.

Scoring Record for Pretests, Posttests, Mid-Test, and Final Test

Pretests, Posttests, Mid-Test, and Final Test	Your Score	Performance			
		Excellent	Very Good	Fair	Needs Improvement
Chapter 1 Pretest	____ of 18	17–18	15–16	11–14	10 or fewer
Chapter 1 Posttest	____ of 21	20–21	17–19	13–16	12 or fewer
Chapter 2 Pretest	____ of 6	6	5	4	3 or fewer
Chapter 2 Posttest	____ of 5	5	4	3	2 or fewer
Chapter 3 Pretest	____ of 19	18–19	15–17	12–14	11 or fewer
Chapter 3 Posttest	____ of 17	16–17	14–15	11–13	10 or fewer
Chapter 4 Pretest	____ of 5	5	4	3	2 or fewer
Chapter 4 Posttest	____ of 4	4	3	2	1
Chapter 5 Pretest	____ of 8	8	6–7	5	4 or fewer
Chapter 5 Posttest	____ of 15	14–15	12–13	9–11	8 or fewer
Chapter 6 Pretest	____ of 4	4	3	2	1
Chapter 6 Posttest	____ of 5	5	4	3	2 or fewer
Chapter 7 Pretest	____ of 30	29–30	25–28	19–24	18 or fewer
Chapter 7 Posttest	____ of 30	29–30	25–28	19–24	18 or fewer
Mid-Test	____ of 20	19–20	16–18	13–15	12 or fewer
Final Test	____ of 69	66–69	56–65	42–55	41 or fewer

Page 5

NAME _____

Check What You Know
Points, Lines, Rays, and Angles

CHAPTER 1 PRETEST

Under each of the following items, write line, line segment, or ray. Then, circle the correct names. Each may have more than one correct name.

1. a line segment JK (JK) (KJ)
   b line (RF) ∠RF (FR)
   c ray QP (QP) (PQ)

Name the angles that have L as their vertex.

2. ∠4   ∠5   ∠KLM

Name ∠5 in two different ways.

∠NLM   ∠MLN

Use the figure to complete the following.

4. Name an angle that is vertical to ∠ABD.   ∠CBH

5. Name an angle that is vertical to ∠GBH.   ∠DBE

6. Name an angle that is supplementary to ∠EBC.   ∠EBA

7. ∠EBC is 90°. BF bisects ∠EBC.
   What is the measure of ∠EBF?   45°

8. Name the angle that is complementary to ∠FBC.   ∠FBE

Spectrum Geometry
Grade 6
5

Chapter 1
Points, Lines, Rays, and Angles

Page 6

NAME _____   SCORE __/8

Points, Lines, and Rays

A **point** has no dimensions but defines a location in space.
Points are usually named by the capital letter. A•
A **line** extends infinitely in both directions.
A line is named by choosing any two points on a line.

Line BC (BC) is the same as line CB (CB).   B——C

A **line segment** is part of a line that begins at one point and ends at another.

Segment DE (DE) is the same as segment ED (ED).   D——E

A **ray** is an infinitely long part of a line that begins at a point called a *vertex*.
To name a ray, choose another point on the ray and name it from its vertex.

This is ray FG (FG). It is not ray GF because G is not its vertex.   F——G

Draw and name the following figures.

1. line AB   A——B   AB

2. ray FG   F——G   FG

3. line segment HK   H——K   HK

4. line segment KH   H——K   KH

Spectrum Geometry
Grade 6
6

Chapter 1
Points, Lines, Rays, and Angles

Page 7

NAME _____   SCORE __/24

Points and Lines

Complete the following.

              a   b
1.   line RS or SR   RS or SR
2.   line PQ or QP   PQ or QP
3.   line MN or NM   MN or NM

              a   b   c
4.   line segment XY or YX   XY or YX   endpoints X and Y
5.   line segment AB or BA   AB or BA   endpoints A and B

Draw the following.

       a   b
6. line TU   OP
    T   U   O   P

7. GH   JK
   G   H   J   K

8. line segment XY   WX
   X   Y   W   X

Spectrum Geometry
Grade 6
7

Chapter 1
Points, Lines, Rays, and Angles

Page 8

NAME _____   SCORE __/9

Measuring Angles

An **angle** (∠) is formed by two rays which have a common vertex.

The angle is named ABC (∠ABC) or CBA (∠CBA). The **vertex**, the point where two rays meet, is always in the middle of the angle name. The measure of ∠ABC is 45°.

If the measure of an angle is less than 90°, it is an acute angle.

If the measure of an angle is 90°, it is a right angle.   This symbol means right angle.   ∠QRS is a right angle.

If the measure of an angle is more than 90°, it is an obtuse angle.   ∠CDF is obtuse. The measure of ∠CDF is 117°.

This angle (∠) is formed by BA and BC.

Name each angle. Write whether it is acute (A), right (R), or obtuse (O). Then, measure the angle.

1. ∠LJK or ∠KJL   R   90°

2. ∠MNO or ∠ONM   A   45°

3. ∠RST or ∠TSR   O   130°

Spectrum Geometry
Grade 6
8

Chapter 1
Points, Lines, Rays, and Angles

Page 9

NAME _____   SCORE __/4

Types of Angles

Vertical angles are formed when two straight lines intersect. They are opposite angles and are equal in measure. ∠A and ∠C are a pair of vertical angles. ∠B and ∠D are also vertical angles.

Two angles are **supplementary** if their sum is 180°. In the figure, ∠X and ∠Y are supplementary angles. The measure of ∠X = 150° and the measure of ∠Y = 30°. If two angles have a common vertex and their sides form a straight line, they are supplementary because a straight line has an angle measure of 180°.

Two angles are **complementary** if their sum is 90°. In the figure, ∠M and ∠N are complementary. The measure of ∠M is 40° and the measure of ∠N is 50°.

An **angle bisector** is a line drawn through the vertex of an angle that divides it into two congruent angles, or angles that have the same measure. In the figure, ray BD bisects ∠ABC so that the measure of ∠ABD is the same as the measure of ∠DBC.

Solve each problem.

1. ∠A and ∠G are vertical angles. The measure of ∠A is 72°, what is the measure of ∠G?   72°

2. ∠Y and ∠Z are supplementary angles. The measure of ∠Y is 112°. What is the measure of ∠Z?   68°

3. ∠A and ∠B are complementary angles. The measure of ∠A is 53°. What is the measure of ∠B?   37°

4. ∠RST is bisected by ray SW. The measure of ∠WST is 30°, what is the measure of ∠RST?   60°

Spectrum Geometry
Grade 6
9

Chapter 1
Points, Lines, Rays, and Angles

Page 10

NAME _____   SCORE __/10

Vertical, Supplementary, and Complementary Angles

Use the figure at the right to answer questions 1–4.

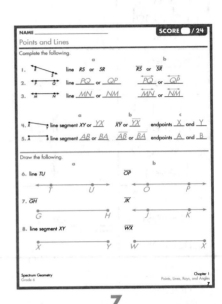

1. Name an angle that is vertical to ∠EHF.   ∠GHJ or ∠GHM

2. Name an angle that is vertical to ∠EHM.   ∠FHG

3. Name an angle that is supplementary to ∠IMJ.   ∠JMK or ∠IMH

4. Name the bisector of ∠HMK.   ML

Use the figure at the right to answer questions 5 and 6.

5. Name an angle complementary to ∠BFC.   ∠CFD

6. Name an angle complementary to ∠AFG.   ∠GFE

Solve.

7. ∠RST is supplementary to angle ∠PSO. The measure of ∠RST is 103°.
   What is the measure of ∠PSO?   77°

8. ∠MNO and ∠NOP are complementary. The measure of ∠NOP is 22°.
   What is the measure of ∠MNO?   68°

9. ∠XYZ is bisected by YW. The measure of ∠XYW is 52°. What is the measure of ∠WYZ? What is the measure of ∠XYZ?
   The measure of ∠WYZ is   52°
   The measure of ∠XYZ is   104°

Spectrum Geometry
Grade 6
10

Chapter 1
Points, Lines, Rays, and Angles

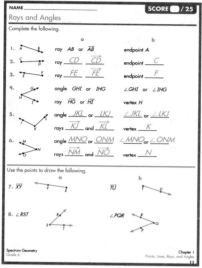

Page 11

NAME _____ SCORE ⬤ / 25

Rays and Angles

Complete the following.

     a   b

1. ray AB or $\overrightarrow{AB}$ endpoint _A_
2. ray _CD_ $\overrightarrow{CD}$ endpoint _C_
3. ray _FE_ $\overrightarrow{FE}$ endpoint _F_
4. angle _GHI_ or _IHG_ $\angle GHI$ or $\angle IHG$
   ray _HG_ or _HI_   vertex _H_
5. angle _JKL_ or _LKJ_ $\angle JKL$ or $\angle LKJ$
   rays _KJ_ and _KL_   vertex _K_
6. angle _MNO_ or _ONM_ $\angle MNO$ or $\angle ONM$
   rays $\overrightarrow{NM}$ and $\overrightarrow{NO}$ vertex _N_

Use the points to draw the following.

     a   b

7. $\overline{XY}$ $\overline{TU}$

8. $\angle RST$ $\angle PQR$

Spectrum Geometry
Grade 6   Chapter 1
Points, Lines, Rays, and Angles

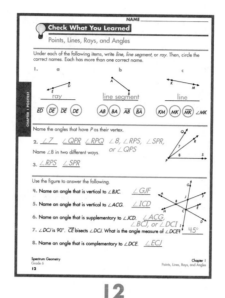

Page 12

NAME _____

💡 Check What You Learned

Points, Lines, Rays, and Angles

Under each of the following items, write *line*, *line segment*, or *ray*. Then, circle the correct names. Each has more than one correct name.

1.   a   b   c

    ray   line segment   line

    ED (DE) DE DE   AB BA (AB) (BA)   KM MK (MK) (MK)

Name the angles that have *P* as their vertex.

2. $\angle 7$ $\angle QPR$ or $\angle RPQ$ $\angle 8$, $\angle RPS$, $\angle SPR$,
   Name $\angle 8$ in two different ways.   or $\angle QPS$

3. $\angle RPS$ $\angle SPR$

Use the figure to answer the following.

4. Name an angle that is vertical to $\angle BJC$. $\angle GJF$
5. Name an angle that is vertical to $\angle ACG$. $\angle ICD$
6. Name an angle that is supplementary to $\angle JCD$. $\angle ACG$, $\angle BCJ$, or $\angle DCI$
7. $\angle DCJ$ is 90°. $\overrightarrow{CE}$ bisects $\angle DCJ$. What is the angle measure of $\angle DCE$?   45°
8. Name an angle that is complementary to $\angle DCE$. $\angle ECJ$

Spectrum Geometry
Grade 6   Chapter 1
Points, Lines, Rays, and Angles

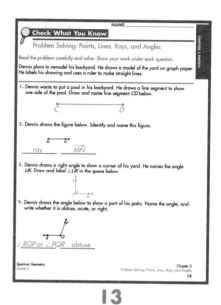

Page 13

NAME _____

🔍 Check What You Know

Problem Solving: Points, Lines, Rays, and Angles

Read the problem carefully and solve. Show your work under each question.

Dennis plans to remodel his backyard. He draws a model of the yard on graph paper. He labels his drawing and uses a ruler to make straight lines.

1. Dennis wants to put a pool in his backyard. He draws a line segment to show one side of the pool. Draw and name line segment *CD* below.

2. Dennis draws the figure below. Identify and name this figure.

    ray $\overrightarrow{MN}$

3. Dennis draws a right angle to show a corner of his yard. He names the angle *LJK*. Draw and label $\angle LJK$ in the space below.

4. Dennis draws the angle below to show a part of his patio. Name the angle, and write whether it is obtuse, acute, or right.

    $\angle RQP$ or $\angle PQR$ obtuse

Spectrum Geometry
Grade 6   Chapter 2
Problem Solving: Points, Lines, Rays, and Angles

Page 14

NAME _____ SCORE ⬤ / 3

Rays and Angles

Read the problem carefully and solve. Show your work under each question.

Alvin is helping to plan a playground for the neighborhood. The playground plan has many rays and angles.

> **Helpful Hint**
> An angle is the union of two rays. The middle of the angle is where the two rays meet.

1. One corner of the playground is represented using the angle shown below. Use geometric notation to name the angle in two ways.

    $\angle ABC$ or $\angle CBA$

2. Alvin draws a ray on the plan that shows the direction people will enter the playground. How would he label ray *MN* on the plans?

    $\overrightarrow{MN}$

Spectrum Geometry
Grade 6   Chapter 2
Problem Solving: Points, Lines, Rays, and Angles

Page 15

NAME _____ SCORE ⬤ / 3

Rays and Angles

3. Alvin combined two rays, $\overrightarrow{BA}$ and $\overrightarrow{BC}$, to make an angle at the edge of the playground plan. Draw and label this angle.

    $\angle ABC$

4. Alvin was asked to draw angle *RQS* to represent the relationship of the slide to the ground. He drew the angle shown below. Did Alvin draw the angle correctly?

    no

5. The gate and the fence in the playground form the angle shown below. Name two geometric figures that are combined to make this angle?

    $\overrightarrow{LK}$, $\overrightarrow{LM}$

Spectrum Geometry
Grade 6   Chapter 2
Problem Solving: Points, Lines, Rays, and Angles

Page 16

NAME _____ SCORE ⬤ / 2

Types of Angles

Read the problem carefully and solve. Show your work under each question.

Keisha makes a map of the streets near her house. She uses angles and intersecting lines to represent the streets. She decides to label the lines and angles on her map. She also plans to measure some of the angles.

> **Helpful Hint**
> **Vertical angles** are formed when two straight lines intersect. They are opposite angles and are equal.
> Two angles are **supplementary** if their sum is 180°.
> Two angles are **complementary** if their sum is 90°.
> An **angle bisector** is a line drawn through the vertex of an angle that divides it into two angles that have the same measure.

1. Keisha measures two supplementary angles, $\angle J$ and $\angle K$, on her map. The measure of $\angle K$ is 124°. What is the measure of $\angle J$?

    56°

2. Keisha draws $\angle RST$ below. She draws $\overrightarrow{SV}$ so that it bisects $\angle RST$. The measure of $\angle VST$ is 25°. What is the measure of $\angle RST$?

    50°

Spectrum Geometry
Grade 6   Chapter 2
Problem Solving: Points, Lines, Rays, and Angles

Answer Key

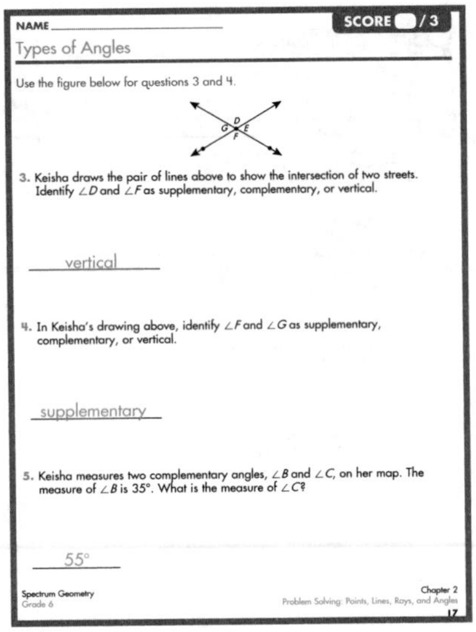

Types of Angles

Use the figure below for questions 3 and 4.

3. Keisha draws the pair of lines above to show the intersection of two streets. Identify ∠D and ∠F as supplementary, complementary, or vertical.

    vertical

4. In Keisha's drawing above, identify ∠F and ∠G as supplementary, complementary, or vertical.

    supplementary

5. Keisha measures two complementary angles, ∠B and ∠C, on her map. The measure of ∠B is 35°. What is the measure of ∠C?

    55°

Spectrum Geometry
Grade 6
Problem Solving: Points, Lines, Rays, and Angles
17

17

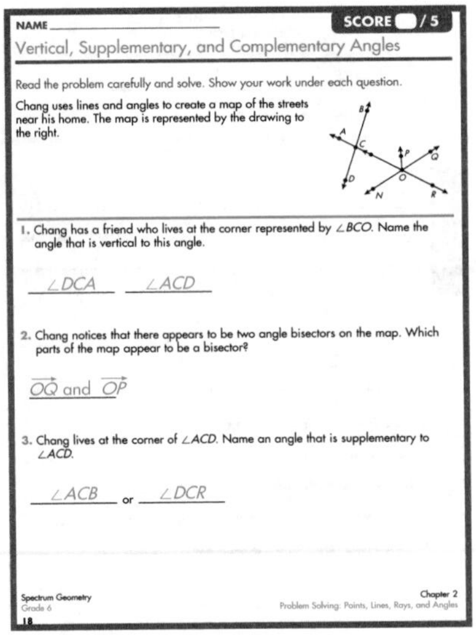

Vertical, Supplementary, and Complementary Angles

Read the problem carefully and solve. Show your work under each question.

Chang uses lines and angles to create a map of the streets near his home. The map is represented by the drawing to the right.

1. Chang has a friend who lives at the corner represented by ∠BCO. Name the angle that is vertical to this angle.

    ∠DCA   **∠ACD**

2. Chang notices that there appears to be two angle bisectors on the map. Which parts of the map appear to be a bisector?

    OQ and OP

3. Chang lives at the corner of ∠ACD. Name an angle that is supplementary to ∠ACD.

    ∠ACB or **∠DCR**

Spectrum Geometry
Grade 6
Problem Solving: Points, Lines, Rays, and Angles
18

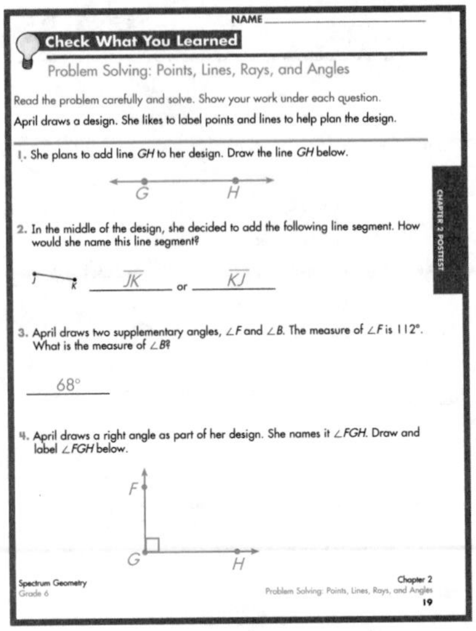

18

Check What You Learned

Problem Solving: Points, Lines, Rays, and Angles

Read the problem carefully and solve. Show your work under each question.

April draws a design. She likes to label points and lines to help plan the design.

1. She plans to add line GH to her design. Draw the line GH below.

    G ——— H

2. In the middle of the design, she decided to add the following line segment. How would she name this line segment?

    JK or **KJ**

3. April draws two supplementary angles, ∠F and ∠B. The measure of ∠F is 112°. What is the measure of ∠B?

    68°

4. April draws a right angle as part of her design. She names it ∠FGH. Draw and label ∠FGH below.

Spectrum Geometry
Grade 6
Problem Solving: Points, Lines, Rays, and Angles
19

19

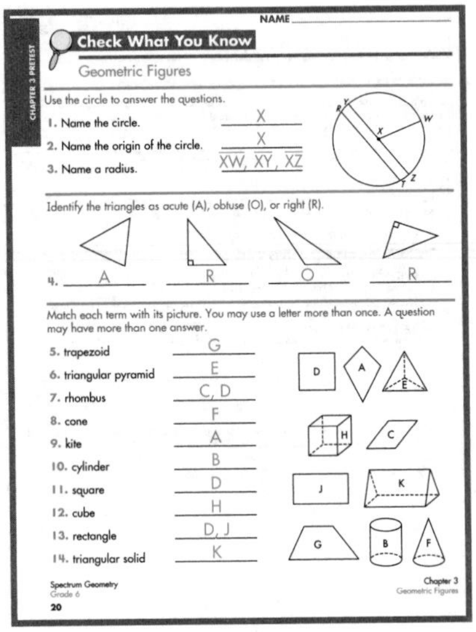

Check What You Know

Geometric Figures

Use the circle to answer the questions.

1. Name the circle.   **X**
2. Name the origin of the circle.   **X**
3. Name a radius.   **XW, XY, XZ**

Identify the triangles as acute (A), obtuse (O), or right (R).

4.   **A**   **R**   **O**   **R**

Match each term with its picture. You may use a letter more than once. A question may have more than one answer.

5. trapezoid   **G**
6. triangular pyramid   **E**
7. rhombus   **C, D**
8. cone   **F**
9. kite   **A**
10. cylinder   **B**
11. square   **D**
12. cube   **H**
13. rectangle   **D, J**
14. triangular solid   **K**

Spectrum Geometry
Grade 6
Chapter 3
Geometric Figures
20

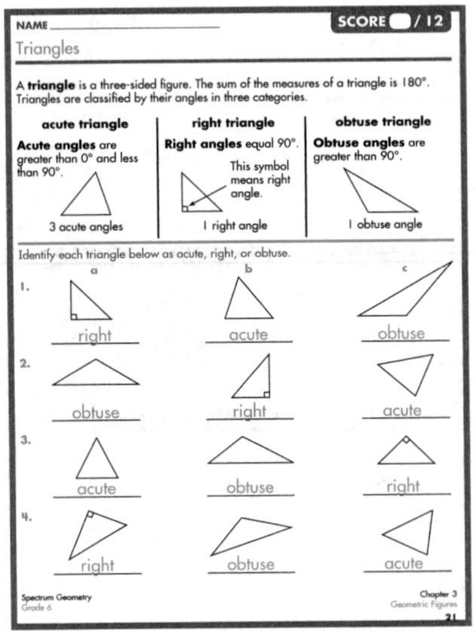

20

Triangles

A **triangle** is a three-sided figure. The sum of the measures of a triangle is 180°. Triangles are classified by their angles in three categories.

acute triangle	right triangle	obtuse triangle
Acute angles are greater than 0° and less than 90°.	**Right angles** equal 90°. This symbol means right angle.	**Obtuse angles** are greater than 90°.
3 acute angles	1 right angle	1 obtuse angle

Identify each triangle below as acute, right, or obtuse.

1.   a **right**   b **acute**   c **obtuse**

2.   **obtuse**   **right**   **acute**

3.   **acute**   **obtuse**   **right**

4.   **right**   **obtuse**   **acute**

Spectrum Geometry
Grade 6
Chapter 3
Geometric Figures
21

21

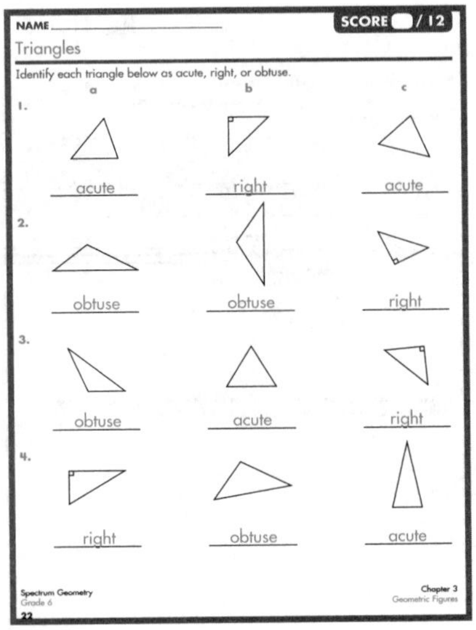

Triangles

Identify each triangle below as acute, right, or obtuse.

1.   a **acute**   b **right**   c **acute**

2.   **obtuse**   **obtuse**   **right**

3.   **obtuse**   **acute**   **right**

4.   **right**   **obtuse**   **acute**

Spectrum Geometry
Grade 6
Chapter 3
Geometric Figures
23

22

Answer Key

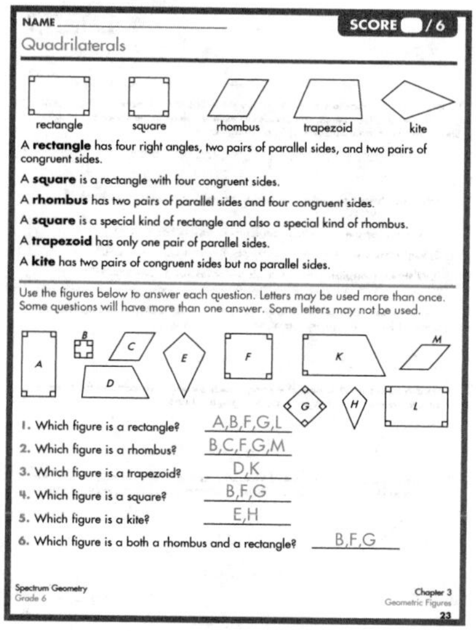

Quadrilaterals

rectangle   square   rhombus   trapezoid   kite

A **rectangle** has four right angles, two pairs of parallel sides, and two pairs of congruent sides.

A **square** is a rectangle with four congruent sides.

A **rhombus** has two pairs of parallel sides and four congruent sides.

A **square** is a special kind of rectangle and also a special kind of rhombus.

A **trapezoid** has only one pair of parallel sides.

A **kite** has two pairs of congruent sides but no parallel sides.

Use the figures below to answer each question. Letters may be used more than once. Some questions will have more than one answer. Some letters may not be used.

1. Which figure is a rectangle? __A,B,F,G,L__
2. Which figure is a rhombus? __B,C,F,G,M__
3. Which figure is a trapezoid? __D,K__
4. Which figure is a square? __B,F,G__
5. Which figure is a kite? __E,H__
6. Which figure is a both a rhombus and a rectangle? __B,F,G__

Spectrum Geometry
Grade 6

Chapter 3
Geometric Figures
23

23

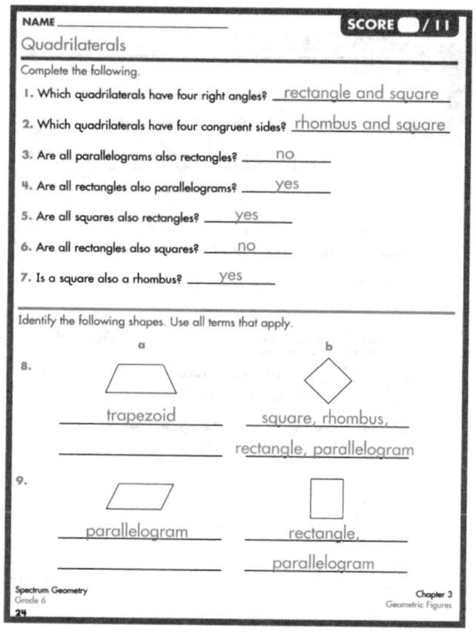

Quadrilaterals

Complete the following.

1. Which quadrilaterals have four right angles? __rectangle and square__
2. Which quadrilaterals have four congruent sides? __rhombus and square__
3. Are all parallelograms also rectangles? __no__
4. Are all rectangles also parallelograms? __yes__
5. Are all squares also rectangles? __yes__
6. Are all rectangles also squares? __no__
7. Is a square also a rhombus? __yes__

Identify the following shapes. Use all terms that apply.

8.
a __trapezoid__
b __square, rhombus, rectangle, parallelogram__

9.
__parallelogram__
__rectangle, parallelogram__

Spectrum Geometry
Grade 6
24

Chapter 3
Geometric Figures

24

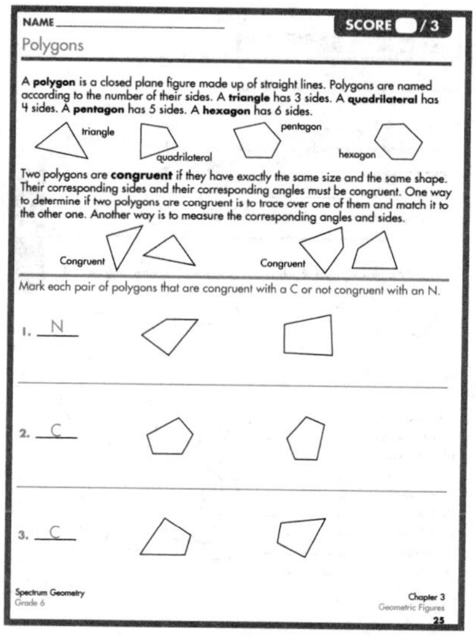

Polygons

A **polygon** is a closed plane figure made up of straight lines. Polygons are named according to the number of their sides. A **triangle** has 3 sides. A **quadrilateral** has 4 sides. A **pentagon** has 5 sides. A **hexagon** has 6 sides.

triangle   quadrilateral   pentagon   hexagon

Two polygons are **congruent** if they have exactly the same size and the same shape. Their corresponding sides and their corresponding angles must be congruent. One way to determine if two polygons are congruent is to trace over one of them and match it to the other one. Another way is to measure the corresponding angles and sides.

Congruent   Congruent

Mark each pair of polygons that are congruent with a C or not congruent with an N.

1. __N__
2. __C__
3. __C__

Spectrum Geometry
Grade 6

Chapter 3
Geometric Figures
25

25

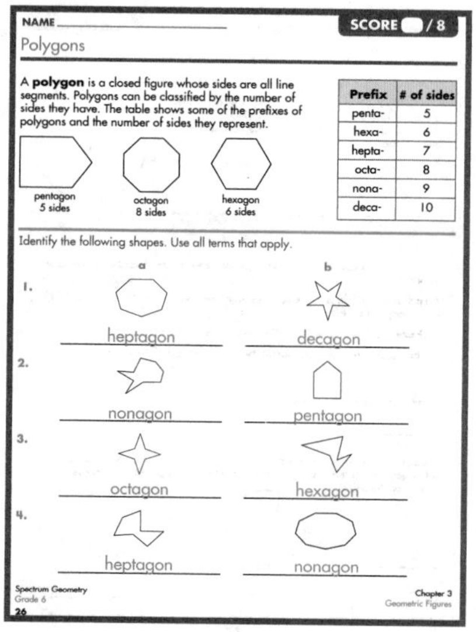

Polygons

A **polygon** is a closed figure whose sides are all line segments. Polygons can be classified by the number of sides they have. The table shows some of the prefixes of polygons and the number of sides they represent.

pentagon   octagon   hexagon
5 sides   8 sides   6 sides

Prefix	# of sides
penta-	5
hexa-	6
hepta-	7
octa-	8
nona-	9
deca-	10

Identify the following shapes. Use all terms that apply.

1.
a __heptagon__
b __decagon__

2.
__nonagon__
__pentagon__

3.
__octagon__
__hexagon__

4.
__heptagon__
__nonagon__

Spectrum Geometry
Grade 6
26

Chapter 3
Geometric Figures

26

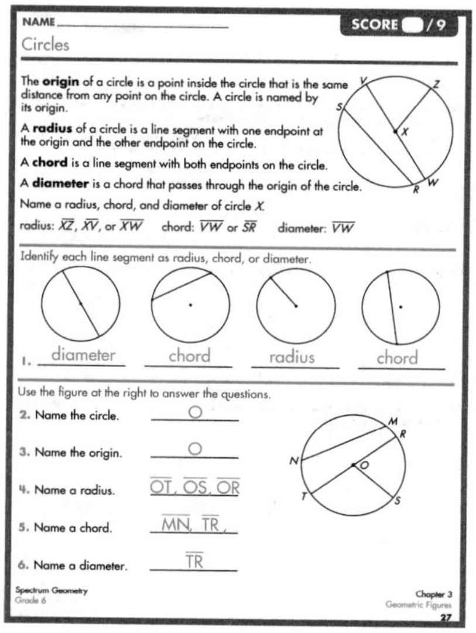

Circles

The **origin** of a circle is a point inside the circle that is the same distance from any point on the circle. A circle is named by its origin.

A **radius** of a circle is a line segment with one endpoint at the origin and the other endpoint on the circle.

A **chord** is a line segment with both endpoints on the circle.

A **diameter** is a chord that passes through the origin of the circle.

Name a radius, chord, and diameter of circle X.

radius: $\overline{XZ}$, $\overline{XV}$, or $\overline{XW}$ chord: $\overline{VW}$ or $\overline{SR}$ diameter: $\overline{VW}$

Identify each line segment as radius, chord, or diameter.

1. __diameter__   __chord__   __radius__   __chord__

Use the figure at the right to answer the questions.

2. Name the circle. __O__
3. Name the origin. __O__
4. Name a radius. __OT, OS, OR__
5. Name a chord. __MN, TR,__
6. Name a diameter. __TR__

Spectrum Geometry
Grade 6

Chapter 3
Geometric Figures
27

27

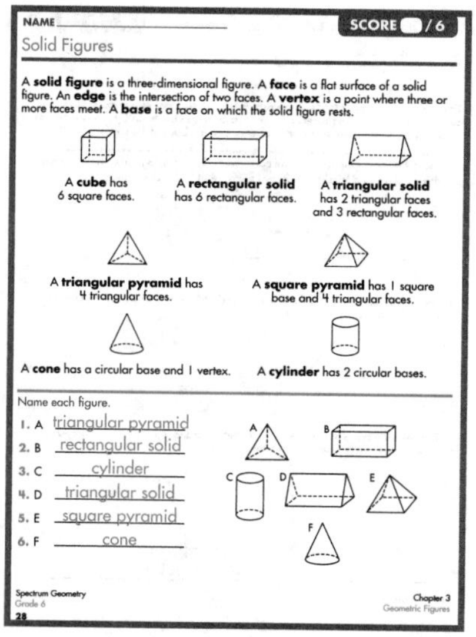

Solid Figures

A **solid figure** is a three-dimensional figure. A **face** is a flat surface of a solid figure. An **edge** is the intersection of two faces. A **vertex** is a point where three or more faces meet. A **base** is a face on which the solid figure rests.

A **cube** has 6 square faces.

A **rectangular solid** has 6 rectangular faces.

A **triangular solid** has 2 triangular faces and 3 rectangular faces.

A **triangular pyramid** has 4 triangular faces.

A **square pyramid** has 1 square base and 4 triangular faces.

A **cone** has a circular base and 1 vertex.

A **cylinder** has 2 circular bases.

Name each figure.

1. A __triangular pyramid__
2. B __rectangular solid__
3. C __cylinder__
4. D __triangular solid__
5. E __square pyramid__
6. F __cone__

Spectrum Geometry
Grade 6
28

Chapter 3
Geometric Figures

28

Spectrum Geometry
Grade 6

Answer Key

87

Answer Key

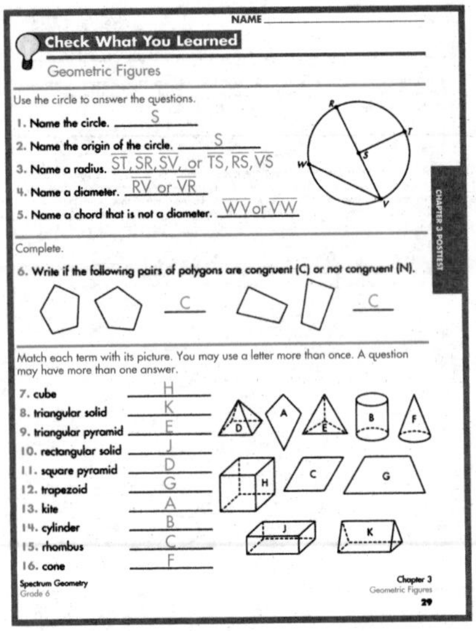

NAME

Check What You Learned

Geometric Figures

Use the circle to answer the questions.

1. Name the circle. ___S___
2. Name the origin of the circle. ___S___
3. Name a radius. ___ST, SR, SV, or TS, RS, VS___
4. Name a diameter. ___RV or VR___
5. Name a chord that is not a diameter. ___WV or VW___

Complete.

6. Write if the following pairs of polygons are congruent (C) or not congruent (N).

___C___   ___C___

Match each term with its picture. You may use a letter more than once. A question may have more than one answer.

7. cube ___H___
8. triangular solid ___K___
9. triangular pyramid ___E___
10. rectangular solid ___J___
11. square pyramid ___D___
12. trapezoid ___G___
13. kite ___A___
14. cylinder ___B___
15. rhombus ___C___
16. cone ___F___

Spectrum Geometry
Grade 6

Chapter 3
Geometric Figures
29

29

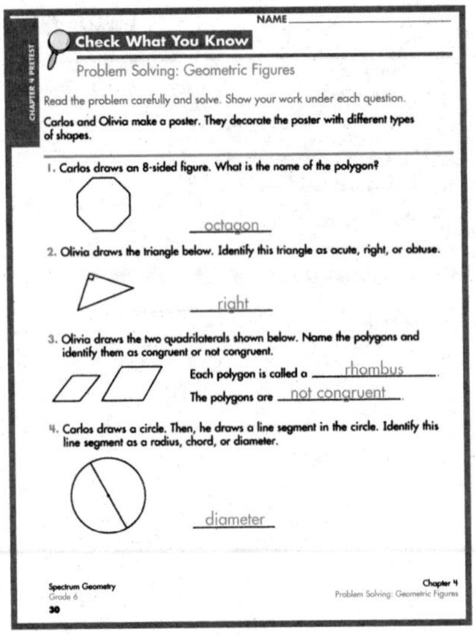

NAME

Check What You Know

Problem Solving: Geometric Figures

Read the problem carefully and solve. Show your work under each question.

Carlos and Olivia make a poster. They decorate the poster with different types of shapes.

1. Carlos draws an 8-sided figure. What is the name of the polygon?

___octagon___

2. Olivia draws the triangle below. Identify this triangle as acute, right, or obtuse.

___right___

3. Olivia draws the two quadrilaterals shown below. Name the polygons and identify them as congruent or not congruent.

Each polygon is called a ___rhombus___
The polygons are ___not congruent___

4. Carlos draws a circle. Then, he draws a line segment in the circle. Identify this line segment as a radius, chord, or diameter.

___diameter___

Spectrum Geometry
Grade 6
30

Chapter 4
Problem Solving: Geometric Figures

30

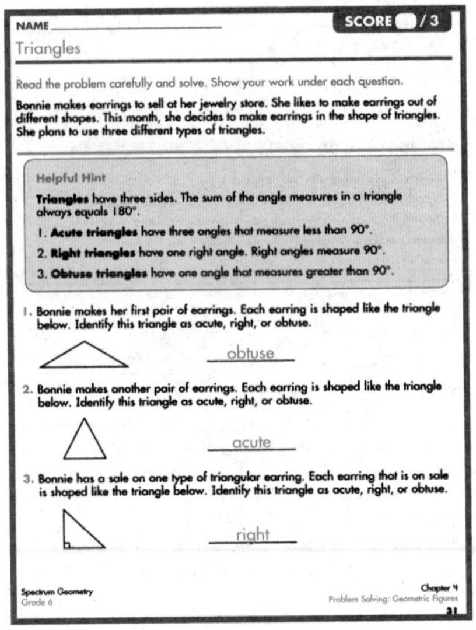

NAME

SCORE / 3

Triangles

Read the problem carefully and solve. Show your work under each question.

Bonnie makes earrings to sell at her jewelry store. She likes to make earrings out of different shapes. This month, she decides to make earrings in the shape of triangles. She plans to use three different types of triangles.

Helpful Hint

Triangles have three sides. The sum of the angle measures in a triangle always equals 180°.

1. **Acute triangles** have three angles that measure less than 90°.
2. **Right triangles** have one right angle. Right angles measure 90°.
3. **Obtuse triangles** have one angle that measures greater than 90°.

1. Bonnie makes her first pair of earrings. Each earring is shaped like the triangle below. Identify this triangle as acute, right, or obtuse.

___obtuse___

2. Bonnie makes another pair of earrings. Each earring is shaped like the triangle below. Identify this triangle as acute, right, or obtuse.

___acute___

3. Bonnie has a sale on one type of triangular earring. Each earring that is on sale is shaped like the triangle below. Identify this triangle as acute, right, or obtuse.

___right___

Spectrum Geometry
Grade 6

Chapter 4
Problem Solving: Geometric Figures
31

31

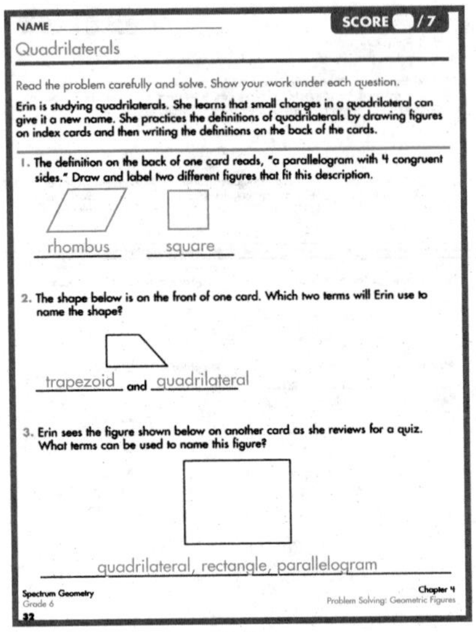

NAME

SCORE / 7

Quadrilaterals

Read the problem carefully and solve. Show your work under each question.

Erin is studying quadrilaterals. She learns that small changes in a quadrilateral can give it a new name. She practices the definitions of quadrilaterals by drawing figures on index cards and then writing the definitions on the back of the cards.

1. The definition on the back of one card reads, "a parallelogram with 4 congruent sides." Draw and label two different figures that fit this description.

___rhombus___   ___square___

2. The shape below is on the front of one card. Which two terms will Erin use to name the shape?

___trapezoid___ and ___quadrilateral___

3. Erin sees the figure shown below on another card as she reviews for a quiz. What terms can be used to name this figure?

___quadrilateral, rectangle, parallelogram___

Spectrum Geometry
Grade 6
32

Chapter 4
Problem Solving: Geometric Figures

32

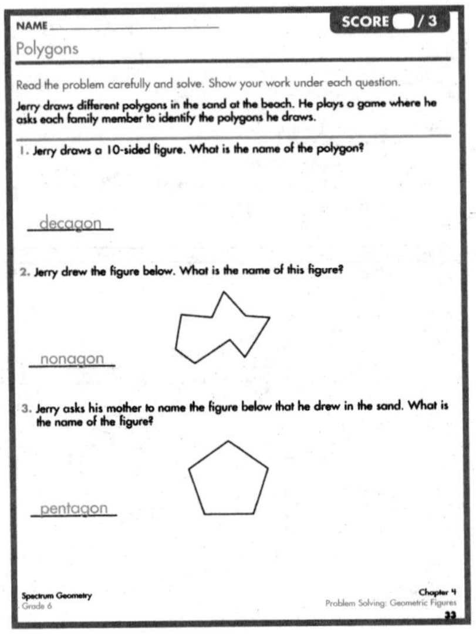

NAME

SCORE / 3

Polygons

Read the problem carefully and solve. Show your work under each question.

Jerry draws different polygons in the sand at the beach. He plays a game where he asks each family member to identify the polygons he draws.

1. Jerry draws a 10-sided figure. What is the name of the polygon?

___decagon___

2. Jerry drew the figure below. What is the name of this figure?

___nonagon___

3. Jerry asks his mother to name the figure below that he drew in the sand. What is the name of the figure?

___pentagon___

Spectrum Geometry
Grade 6
33

Chapter 4
Problem Solving: Geometric Figures
33

33

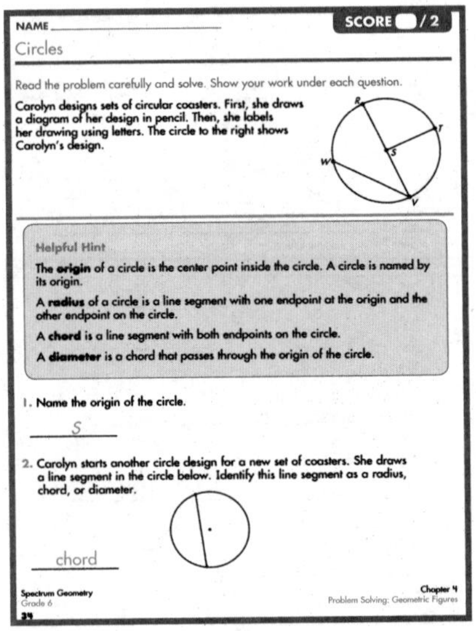

NAME

SCORE / 2

Circles

Read the problem carefully and solve. Show your work under each question.

Carolyn designs sets of circular coasters. First, she draws a diagram of her design in pencil. Then, she labels her drawing using letters. The circle to the right shows Carolyn's design.

Helpful Hint

The **origin** of a circle is the center point inside the circle. A circle is named by its origin.

A **radius** of a circle is a line segment with one endpoint at the origin and the other endpoint on the circle.

A **chord** is a line segment with both endpoints on the circle.

A **diameter** is a chord that passes through the origin of the circle.

1. Name the origin of the circle.

___S___

2. Carolyn starts another circle design for a new set of coasters. She draws a line segment in the circle below. Identify this line segment as a radius, chord, or diameter.

___chord___

Spectrum Geometry
Grade 6
34

Chapter 4
Problem Solving: Geometric Figures

34

Answer Key

NAME _____ **SCORE** ⬭ /3

Circles

3. Name a diameter in Carolyn's circle design. If there is more than one, list them all.

$\overline{RV}$ or $\overline{VR}$

4. Name a radius in the circle. If there is more than one, list them all.

$\overline{SR}$, $\overline{ST}$, $\overline{SV}$ or $\overline{RS}$, $\overline{TS}$, $\overline{VS}$

5. Name a chord in Carolyn's circle that is not a diameter.

$\overline{WV}$ or $\overline{VW}$

Spectrum Geometry
Grade 6
Chapter 4
Problem Solving: Geometric Figures
35

35

NAME _____ **SCORE** ⬭ /4

Solid Figures

Read the problem carefully and solve. Show your work under each question.

Masako plans to use the solid figures below in a model that he will build for a school project. Before he starts, he decides to keep track of the number of **faces**, **vertices**, and **edges** for each solid.

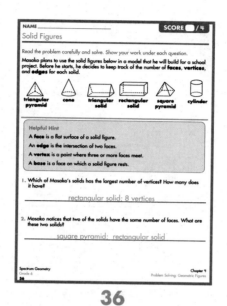

triangular pyramid   cone   triangular solid   rectangular solid   square pyramid   cylinder

Helpful Hint
A **face** is a flat surface of a solid figure.
An **edge** is the intersection of two faces.
A **vertex** is a point where three or more faces meet.
A **base** is a face on which a solid figure rests.

1. Which of Masako's solids has the largest number of vertices? How does it have?

rectangular solid; 8 vertices

2. Masako notices that two of the solids have the same number of faces. What are these two solids?

square pyramid; rectangular solid

Spectrum Geometry
Grade 6
Chapter 4
Problem Solving: Geometric Figures
36

36

NAME _____ **SCORE** ⬭ /3

Solid Figures

3. How many more edges does a square pyramid have than a triangular pyramid?

2 more

4. One of Masako's solids has no vertices. Which one is it?

cylinder

5. The first shape Masako is going to use in his model has only one vertex and a circular base. What is the name of this solid?

cone

Spectrum Geometry
Grade 6
Chapter 4
Problem Solving: Geometric Figures
37

37

NAME _____ **SCORE** ⬭ /4

Quadrilaterals and Polygons

Read the problem carefully and solve. Show your work under each question.

Joanne and Natalia make a quilt with seven different types of polygons cut out of cloth. Before they start, they sort the polygons below in a variety of ways. They give each type of polygon a letter to make the sorting easier.

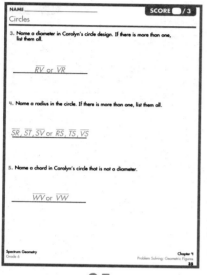

1. Natalia sorts all the polygons to find the ones that are rectangles. Write the letters of the polygons that are rectangles.

A, D, G

2. Natalia cuts out the two polygons below from purple cloth. Name the polygons and identify them as congruent or not congruent.

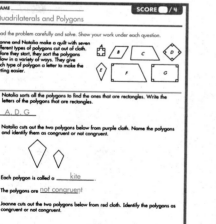

Each polygon is called a ___kite___.

The polygons are _not congruent_

3. Joanne cuts out the two polygons below from red cloth. Identify the polygons as congruent or not congruent.

congruent

Spectrum Geometry
Grade 6
Chapter 4
Problem Solving: Geometric Figures
38

38

NAME _____

💡 **Check What You Learned**

Problem Solving: Geometric Figures

Read the problem carefully and solve. Show your work under each question.

Masako builds a model for his school project. He decides to use polygons and circles as well as solid figures in his model.

1. Masako's model has nine sides. What is the name of the polygon?

nonagon

2. Masako draws the triangle below. Identify this triangle as acute, right, or obtuse.

obtuse

3. Masako draws a polygon with seven sides. What is the name of this polygon?

heptagon

4. Masako draws a line segment in the circle. Identify this line segment as a radius, chord, or diameter in the circle below.

radius

Spectrum Geometry
Grade 6
Chapter 4
Problem Solving: Geometric Figures
39

CHAPTER 4 POSTTEST

39

NAME _____

Mid-Test Chapters 1–4

Draw and name the following figures.

1. line CD $\overleftrightarrow{CD}$
   line segment DC $\overline{DC}$

Name each figure.

2.

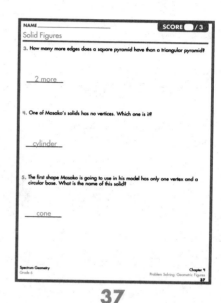

triangular pyramid   cone   rectangular solid

Use the circle to answer the questions.

3. Name the circle.   P
4. The origin of the circle is   P
5. A radius of the circle is $\overline{PQ}$, $\overline{PR}$, or $\overline{PS}$
6. A diameter of the circle is $\overline{RS}$
7. Specify a chord that is not a diameter. $\overline{XW}$ or $\overline{WX}$

Answer the questions about the angles below. ∠m = 55°, ∠x = 35°

8. ∠Y = ___145°___
9. ∠Z = ___35°___
10. ∠W = ___145°___
11. ∠N = ___35°___

Spectrum Geometry
Grade 6
Mid-Test
Chapter 1–4
40

40

Spectrum Geometry
Grade 6

Answer Key

89

Answer Key

Page 41

Read the problem carefully and solve. Show your work under each question.

Jamal makes a design for a new park. The park will have a bricked area with picnic tables, gardens, and walking paths. He draws and labels a blueprint of the picnic area on a coordinate grid for the construction workers. He also draws a map of the park showing the gardens and the walking paths.

12. Jamal wants to cover part of the picnic area with a roof. The roof is shaped like the solid figure below. How many faces does it have?

   5 faces

13. Jamal adds a circular garden to the map of the park. He will plant bushes on part of the garden and flowers on the other part. He draws a line segment in the circle below to show the two sides of the garden. Identify this line segment as a radius, chord, or diameter.

   chord

14. Jamal draws straight lines on the map to represent two walking paths that intersect. This intersection forms two supplementary angles. He labels these two supplementary angles, ∠L and ∠M. The measure of ∠L is 138°. What is the measure of ∠M?

   42°

15. Jamal draws another garden in the shape of the triangle shown below. Identify this triangle as acute, right, or obtuse.

   acute

Spectrum Geometry
Grade 6

Mid-Test
Chapter 1-4
41

41

Page 42

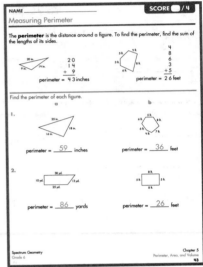

Check What You Know
Perimeter, Area, and Volume

Find the perimeter of each figure.

1.
   perimeter = 89 inches
   perimeter = 139 feet

Find the area of each right triangle.

2.
   area = 315 square inches
   area = 76½ square feet

Find the volume of each rectangular solid.

3.
   volume = 980 cubic yards
   volume = 11,200 cubic feet

Find the surface area of each figure.

4.
   812 sq. in.
   182 sq. cm

Spectrum Geometry
Grade 6
42

Chapter 5
Perimeter, Area, and Volume

42

Page 43

NAME _____   SCORE ___ / 4
Measuring Perimeter

The **perimeter** is the distance around a figure. To find the perimeter, find the sum of the lengths of its sides.

   20   4
   14   8
 + 9   6
            3
           +5
perimeter = 43 inches   perimeter = 26 feet

Find the perimeter of each figure.

        a   b
1.
   perimeter = 59 inches   perimeter = 36 feet

2.
   perimeter = 86 yards   perimeter = 26 feet

Spectrum Geometry
Grade 6

Chapter 5
Perimeter, Area, and Volume
43

43

Page 44

NAME _____   SCORE ___ / 12
Perimeter

Find the perimeter of each figure.

        a   b   c
1.
   14 ft.   13 yd.   12.5 m

2.
   7¼ in.   64 cm   45 yd.

3.
   44 ft.   9 m   12 in.

4.
   12 m   19.2 cm   80 yd.

Spectrum Geometry
Grade 6
44

Chapter 5
Perimeter, Area, and Volume

44

Page 45

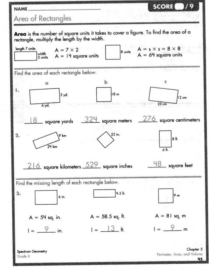

NAME _____   SCORE ___ / 9
Area of Rectangles

Area is the number of square units it takes to cover a figure. To find the area of a rectangle, multiply the length by the width.

length 7 units
width 2 units   A = 7 × 2   A = s × s = 8 × 8
                 A = 14 square units A = 64 square units

Find the area of each rectangle below.

        a   b   c
1.
   18 square yards   324 square meters   276 square centimeters

2.
   216 square kilometers   529 square inches   48 square feet

Find the missing length of each rectangle below.

3.
   A = 54 sq. in.   A = 58.5 sq. ft.   A = 81 sq. m
   l = 9 in.   l = 13 ft.   l = 9 m

Spectrum Geometry
Grade 6

Chapter 5
Perimeter, Area, and Volume
45

45

Page 46

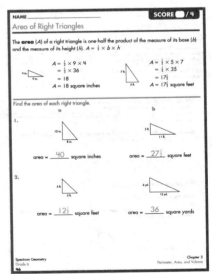

NAME _____   SCORE ___ / 4
Area of Right Triangles

The **area** (A) of a right triangle is one-half the product of the measure of its base (b) and the measure of its height (h). A = ½ × b × h

   A = ½ × 9 × 4   A = ½ × 5 × 7
     = ½ × 36   = ½ × 35
     = 18   = 17½
   A = 18 square inches A = 17½ square feet

Find the area of each right triangle.

        a   b
1.
   area = 40 square inches   area = 27½ square feet

2.
   area = 12½ square feet   area = 36 square yards

Spectrum Geometry
Grade 6
46

Chapter 5
Perimeter, Area, and Volume

46

Answer Key

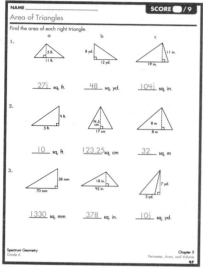

47

NAME _____ SCORE ●/9
Area of Triangles

Find the area of each right triangle.

a	b	c
1. 5 ft. / 11 ft.	8 yd. / 12 yd.	11 in. / 19 in.
$27\frac{1}{2}$ sq. ft.	48 sq. yd.	$104\frac{1}{2}$ sq. in.
2. 4 ft. / 5 ft.	14.5 / 17 cm	8 m / 8 m
10 sq. ft.	123.25 sq. cm	32 sq. m
3. 38 / 70 mm	18 in. / 42 in.	7 yd. / 3 yd.
1330 sq. mm	378 sq. in.	$10\frac{1}{2}$ sq. yd.

Spectrum Geometry
Grade 6
Chapter 5
Perimeter, Area, and Volume
47

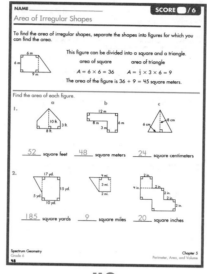

48

NAME _____ SCORE ●/6
Area of Irregular Shapes

To find the area of irregular shapes, separate the shapes into figures for which you can find the area.

This figure can be divided into a square and a triangle.
area of square   area of triangle
$A = 6 \times 6 = 36$ $A = \frac{1}{2} \times 3 \times 6 = 9$
The area of the figure is $36 + 9 = 45$ square meters.

Find the area of each figure.

a	b	c
1. 10 ft. / 8 ft. / 3 ft.	12 m / 8 m / 3 m	6 cm / 8 cm
52 square feet	48 square meters	24 square centimeters
2. 17 yd. / 15 yd. / 5 yd. / 10 yd.	4 mi. / 3 mi. / 2 mi.	2 in. / 2 in. / 2 in.
185 square yards	9 square miles	20 square inches

Spectrum Geometry
Grade 6
48
Chapter 5
Perimeter, Area, and Volume

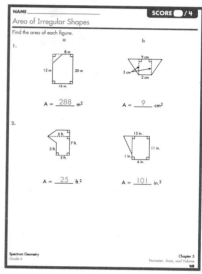

49

NAME _____ SCORE ●/4
Area of Irregular Shapes

Find the area of each figure.

a	b
1. 8 m / 12 m / 20 m / 16 m	4 m / 3 cm / 2 cm
A = 288 m²	A = 9 cm²
2. 5 ft. / 3 ft. / 7 ft. / 3 ft.	13 in. / 1 in. / 11 in.
A = 25 ft.²	A = 101 in.²

Spectrum Geometry
Grade 6
Chapter 5
Perimeter, Area, and Volume
49

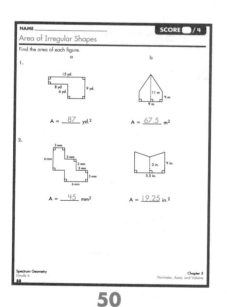

50

NAME _____ SCORE ●/4
Area of Irregular Shapes

Find the area of each figure.

a	b
1. 15 yd. / 8 yd. / 6 yd. / 9 yd.	11 m / 4 m / 9 m
A = 87 yd.²	A = 67.5 m²
2. 3 mm / 3 mm / 6 mm / 3 mm / 3 mm / 6 mm	3 in. / 4 in. / 5.5 in.
A = 45 mm²	A = 19.25 in.²

Spectrum Geometry
Grade 6
50
Chapter 5
Perimeter, Area, and Volume

51

NAME _____ SCORE ●/6
Surface Area of a Rectangular Solid

The **surface area** of a solid is the sum of the areas of all the faces (or surfaces) of the solid. A rectangular solid has six surfaces.

The area of each surface is determined by finding length × width, length × height, and width × height. Calculate the total surface area using the formula $SA = 2lw + 2lh + 2wh$.

In the figure on the left, $l = 1.5$ ft., $w = 1.2$ ft., and $h = 1.6$ ft.
$SA = 2(1.5\text{ ft.})(1.2\text{ ft.}) + 2(1.5\text{ ft.})(1.6\text{ ft.}) + 2(1.2\text{ ft.})(1.6\text{ ft.})$
$SA = 3.6\text{ ft.}^2 + 4.8\text{ ft.}^2 + 3.82\text{ ft.}^2$
$SA = 12.22\text{ ft.}^2$

Find the surface area of each figure.

a	b
1. 3.2 cm / 1.8 cm	20 in. / 12.5 in. / 36 in.
SA = 21.52 cm²	SA = 2840 in.²
2. 6 yd. / 7 yd. / 3 yd.	5 m / 2 m
SA = 214 yd.²	SA = 104 m²
3. 3 mm / 4 mm / 6 mm	4.1 ft. / 4.3 ft. / 10 ft.
SA = 108 mm²	SA = 203.26 ft.²

Spectrum Geometry
Grade 6
Chapter 5
Perimeter, Area, and Volume
51

52

NAME _____ SCORE ●/9
Surface Area of a Rectangular Solid

Find the surface area of each figure.

a	b	c
1. 2 in. / 3 in. / 5 in.	1.3 ft. / 1.5 ft. / 8 ft.	2 ft. / 7 ft. / 8 ft.
62 square inches	48.7 square feet	172 square yards
2. 12 cm / 14 cm / 10 cm	5 m / 6 m / 2 m	6 in. / 14 in.
856 square centimeters	104 square meters	248 square inches
3. 6.5 ft. / 3.5 ft.	20 mm / 38 mm / 12.5 mm	3.2 cm / 6.6 cm
85.5 square feet	2970 square millimeters	81.44 square centimeters

Spectrum Geometry
Grade 6
52
Chapter 5
Perimeter, Area, and Volume

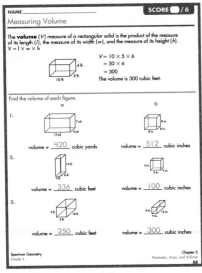

53 — Measuring Volume

The **volume** (V) measure of a rectangular solid is the product of the measure of its length (l), the measure of its width (w), and the measure of its height (h).
$V = l \times w \times h$

$V = 10 \times 5 \times 6$
$= 50 \times 6$
$= 300$
The volume is 300 cubic feet.

Find the volume of each figure.

a | b
1. volume = 420 cubic yards | volume = 512 cubic inches
2. volume = 336 cubic feet | volume = 100 cubic inches
3. volume = 250 cubic feet | volume = 300 cubic inches

Spectrum Geometry Grade 6 — Chapter 5 Perimeter, Area, and Volume — 53

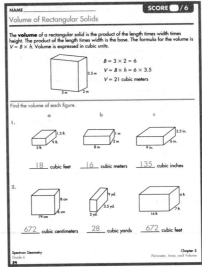

54 — Volume of Rectangular Solids

The **volume** of a rectangular solid is the product of the length times width times height. The product of the length times width is the base. The formula for the volume is $V = B \times h$. Volume is expressed in cubic units.

$B = 3 \times 2 = 6$
$V = B \times h = 6 \times 3.5$
$V = 21$ cubic meters

Find the volume of each figure.

a | b | c
1. 18 cubic feet | 16 cubic meters | 135 cubic inches
2. 672 cubic centimeters | 28 cubic yards | 672 cubic feet

Spectrum Geometry Grade 6 — Chapter 5 Perimeter, Area, and Volume — 54

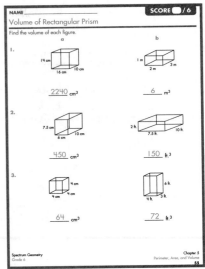

55 — Volume of Rectangular Prism

Find the volume of each figure.

a | b
1. 2240 cm³ | 6 m³
2. 450 cm³ | 150 ft.³
3. 64 cm³ | 72 ft.³

Spectrum Geometry Grade 6 — Chapter 5 Perimeter, Area, and Volume — 55

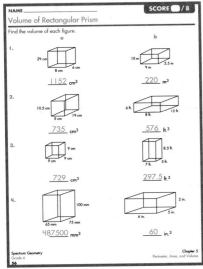

56 — Volume of Rectangular Prism

Find the volume of each figure.

a | b
1. 1152 cm³ | 220 m³
2. 735 cm³ | 576 ft.³
3. 729 cm³ | 297.5 ft.³
4. 487500 mm³ | 60 in.³

Spectrum Geometry Grade 6 — Chapter 5 Perimeter, Area, and Volume — 56

57 — Check What You Learned
Perimeter and Area

Find the perimeter of each figure.

a | b | c
1. $P =$ 24 cm | $P =$ 16 m | $P =$ 28 in.

Find the unknown measure, area, or perimeter.

2. $A = 196$ m²; $s =$ 14 m; $P =$ 56 m | $A =$ 41.25 yd.²; $P =$ 26 yd. | $A =$ 323 mm²; $P =$ 96 mm

Find the area for the parallelograms and irregular shapes.

3. $A =$ 272 ft.² | $A =$ 404 cm² | $A =$ 29.25 yd.²

Find the volume of each rectangular prism.

4. 64 cm³ | 72 ft.³ | 60 in.³

Spectrum Geometry Grade 6 — Chapter 5 Perimeter, Area, and Volume — 57

58 — Check What You Know
Problem Solving: Perimeter, Area, and Volume

Read the problem carefully and solve. Show your work under each question.

Greg spends a week over the summer at an overnight camp. He records many things about his environment while at camp.

1. The layout of the camp is represented by the drawing shown below. There is a fence around the property. How long is the fence?
120 yards

2. The pool has a length of 12 feet, width of 8 feet, and a depth of 5 feet. How much water can the pool hold?
480 cubic feet

3. Greg makes a clay slate in one of his activities at camp. The picture below shows the slate. What is the area of the slate?
104 square inches

4. Greg makes the following object while at camp and wants to paint its sides. What is the surface area of the object?
152 square inches

Spectrum Geometry Grade 6 — Chapter 6 Problem Solving: Perimeter, Area, and Volume — 58

Answer Key

NAME _____ **SCORE** ⬤ / 3

Perimeter

Read the problem carefully and solve. Show your work under each question.

Joanna works for a fencing company. Her job is to determine the amount of fencing needed for various clients.

> **Helpful Hint**
> The **perimeter** of a figure is the sum of the lengths of its sides. If two or more sides are equal, the formula can be simplified with multiplication.

1. Joanna needs to determine the perimeter of an animal pen. How many yards is the perimeter of the pen?

   __340__ yards

2. The figure below represents a city park in the shape of a regular pentagon. The city puts a fence around the park. How many yards of fencing is needed?

   __150__ yards

3. A parking lot is represented by the rectangle below. Joanna's company is hired to put a fence around the lot. How many yards of fencing will be needed?

   __130__ yards

Spectrum Geometry
Grade 6

Problem Solving: Perimeter, Area, and Volume
59

59

NAME _____ **SCORE** ⬤ / 3

Area of Rectangles

Read the problem carefully and solve. Show your work under each question.

Ivan sells rugs that are either square or rectangular in shape. He prices the rugs based on their square footage.

1. Ivan sells the rug below to a new customer. What is the area of this rug?

   __35__ square yards

2. The most popular rug that Ivan sells is represented by the figure below. A customer at the store wants to know the area of this rug. Write the area below.

   __120__ square feet

3. On Saturday, Ivan sells a large rug to a restaurant. The rug measures 24 feet by 18 feet. What is the area of the rug?

   __432__ square feet

Spectrum Geometry
Grade 6

Problem Solving: Perimeter, Area, and Volume
60

60

NAME _____ **SCORE** ⬤ / 3

Area of Triangles

Read the problem carefully and solve. Show your work under each question.

Hugo makes ceramic tiles that are triangular in shape. He sells his tiles to friends and businesses in the town where he lives.

1. One type of tile Hugo makes that is often purchased for kitchen counters is shown below. Find the area of the tile.

   __540__ square millimeters

2. Hugo makes tiles for his mother in the shape shown below. She plans to use them in her living room. What is the area of each tile?

   __150__ square centimeters

3. Hugo makes a pattern using only tiles like the one shown below. He wants to know how many tiles can fit on the counter where he is building out the pattern. Find the area of each tile.

   __6__ square inches

Spectrum Geometry
Grade 6

Problem Solving: Perimeter, Area, and Volume
61

61

NAME _____ **SCORE** ⬤ / 2

Surface Area

Read the problem carefully and solve. Show your work under each question.

Mr. Benson sells packaging boxes. The boxes come in a variety of sizes.

> **Helpful Hint**
> The **surface area** of a solid is the sum of the areas of all the faces (or surfaces of the solid). The surface area of a rectangular solid can be found by the formula $SA = 2lw + 2lh + 2wh$.

1. The picture below represents the building that Mr. Benson works in. The surface area of the building is 416 square yards. What is the height of the building?

   __4__ yards

2. Mr. Benson buys a jewelry box for his daughter. The box measures 7 inches by 5 inches by 3 inches. What is the surface area of the box?

   __142__ square inches

Spectrum Geometry
Grade 6

Problem Solving: Perimeter, Area, and Volume
62

62

NAME _____ **SCORE** ⬤ / 3

Surface Area

1. The most popular-sized box Mr. Benson sells has the dimensions of 32 cm by 12 cm by 26 cm. What is the surface area of this box?

   __3056__ square centimeters

2. Mr. Benson has a customer who wants to know the surface area of the box below so she can buy enough gift-wrap for the box. What is the surface area of the box?

   __88__ square inches

3. One of Mr. Benson's customers buys the box below to send some books through the mail. What is the surface area of the box?

   __488__ square inches

Spectrum Geometry
Grade 6

Problem Solving: Perimeter, Area, and Volume
63

63

NAME _____ **SCORE** ⬤ / 3

Area of Irregular Shapes

Read the problem carefully and solve. Show your work under each question.

Olivia learns about irregular shapes in school. Then, she begins to notice all sorts of irregular shapes in the world around her.

1. Olivia looks at a drawing of her parents' property and then draws the shape below to represent it. What is the area of the property?

   __1200__ square meters

2. Olivia's family has a cottage by a lake. The picture below shows the layout of the cottage. What is the area?

   __216__ square yards

3. Olivia finds a plastic shape in her house that has the dimensions shown below. What is the area of the shape?

   __80__ square inches

Spectrum Geometry
Grade 6

Problem Solving: Perimeter, Area, and Volume
64

64

Spectrum Geometry
Grade 6

Answer Key

Answer Key

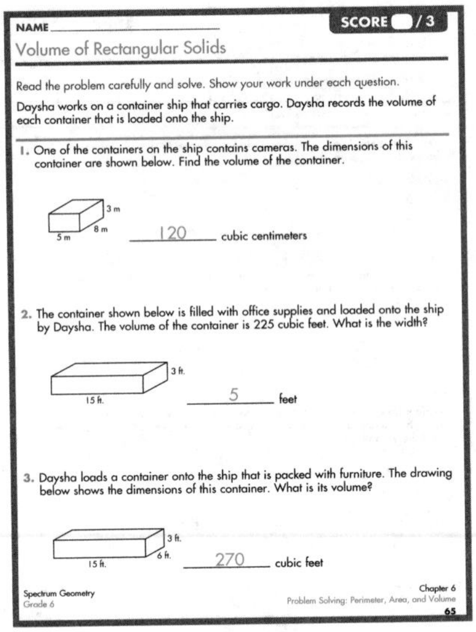
NAME ______ SCORE ___ /3

Volume of Rectangular Solids

Read the problem carefully and solve. Show your work under each question.

Daysha works on a container ship that carries cargo. Daysha records the volume of each container that is loaded onto the ship.

1. One of the containers on the ship contains cameras. The dimensions of this container are shown below. Find the volume of the container.

3 m, 8 m, 5 m — 120 cubic centimeters

2. The container shown below is filled with office supplies and loaded onto the ship by Daysha. The volume of the container is 225 cubic feet. What is the width?

3 ft., 15 ft. — 5 feet

3. Daysha loads a container onto the ship that is packed with furniture. The drawing below shows the dimensions of this container. What is its volume?

3 ft., 6 ft., 15 ft. — 270 cubic feet

Spectrum Geometry Grade 6 — Chapter 6 Problem Solving: Perimeter, Area, and Volume 65

65

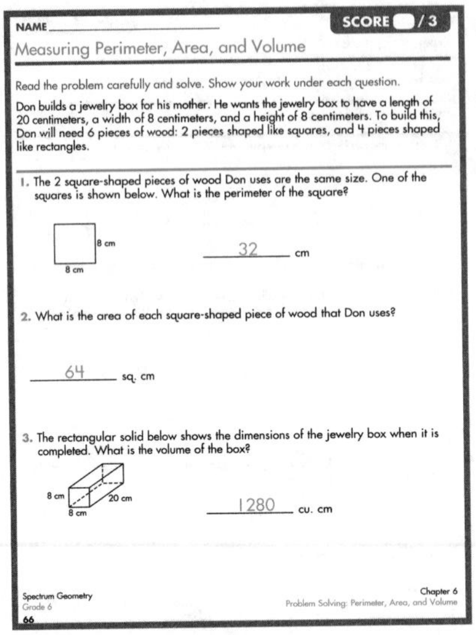
NAME ______ SCORE ___ /3

Measuring Perimeter, Area, and Volume

Read the problem carefully and solve. Show your work under each question.

Don builds a jewelry box for his mother. He wants the jewelry box to have a length of 20 centimeters, a width of 8 centimeters, and a height of 8 centimeters. To build this, Don will need 6 pieces of wood: 2 pieces shaped like squares, and 4 pieces shaped like rectangles.

1. The 2 square-shaped pieces of wood Don uses are the same size. One of the squares is shown below. What is the perimeter of the square?

8 cm, 8 cm — 32 cm

2. What is the area of each square-shaped piece of wood that Don uses?

64 sq. cm

3. The rectangular solid below shows the dimensions of the jewelry box when it is completed. What is the volume of the box?

8 cm, 8 cm, 20 cm — 1280 cu. cm

Spectrum Geometry Grade 6 66 — Chapter 6 Problem Solving: Perimeter, Area, and Volume

66

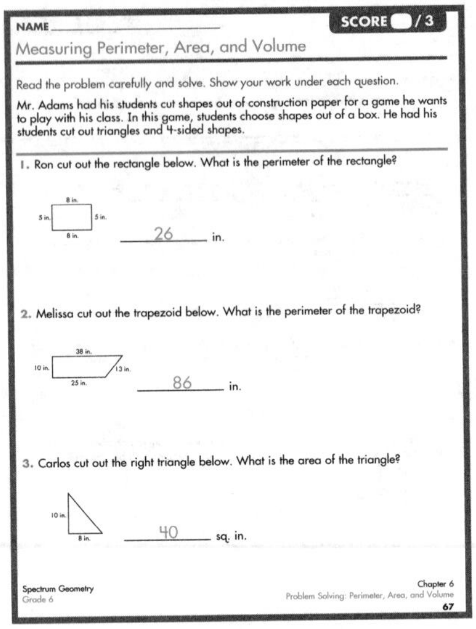
NAME ______ SCORE ___ /3

Measuring Perimeter, Area, and Volume

Read the problem carefully and solve. Show your work under each question.

Mr. Adams had his students cut shapes out of construction paper for a game he wants to play with his class. In this game, students choose shapes out of a box. He had his students cut out triangles and 4-sided shapes.

1. Ron cut out the rectangle below. What is the perimeter of the rectangle?

8 in., 5 in., 5 in., 8 in. — 26 in.

2. Melissa cut out the trapezoid below. What is the perimeter of the trapezoid?

38 in., 10 in., 13 in., 25 in. — 86 in.

3. Carlos cut out the right triangle below. What is the area of the triangle?

10 in., 8 in. — 40 sq. in.

Spectrum Geometry Grade 6 — Chapter 6 Problem Solving: Perimeter, Area, and Volume 67

67

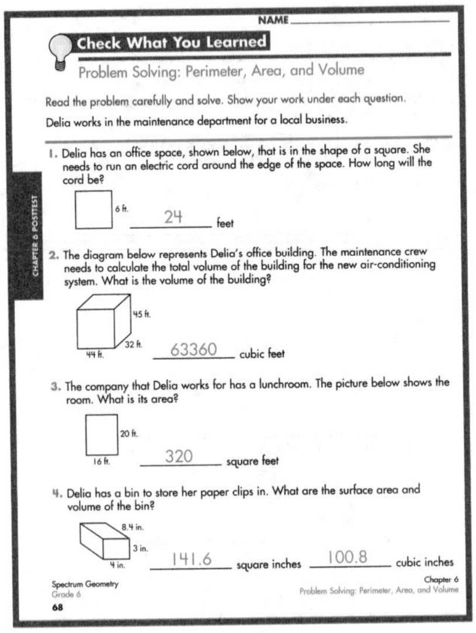
NAME ______

Check What You Learned

Problem Solving: Perimeter, Area, and Volume

CHAPTER 6 POSTTEST

Read the problem carefully and solve. Show your work under each question.

Delia works in the maintenance department for a local business.

1. Delia has an office space, shown below, that is in the shape of a square. She needs to run an electric cord around the edge of the space. How long will the cord be?

6 ft. — 24 feet

2. The diagram below represents Delia's office building. The maintenance crew needs to calculate the total volume of the building for the new air-conditioning system. What is the volume of the building?

45 ft., 32 ft., 44 ft. — 63360 cubic feet

3. The company that Delia works for has a lunchroom. The picture below shows the room. What is its area?

20 ft., 16 ft. — 320 square feet

4. Delia has a bin to store her paper clips in. What are the surface area and volume of the bin?

8.4 in., 3 in., 4 in. — 141.6 square inches 100.8 cubic inches

Spectrum Geometry Grade 6 68 — Chapter 6 Problem Solving: Perimeter, Area, and Volume

68

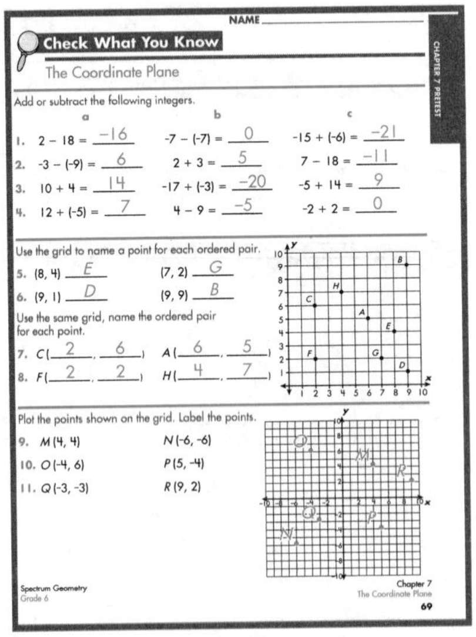
NAME ______

Check What You Know

The Coordinate Plane

CHAPTER 7 PRETEST

Add or subtract the following integers.

	a	b	c
1.	2 − 18 = −16	−7 − (−7) = 0	−15 + (−6) = −21
2.	−3 − (−9) = 6	2 + 3 = 5	7 − 18 = −11
3.	10 + 4 = 14	−17 + (−3) = −20	−5 + 14 = 9
4.	12 + (−5) = 7	4 − 9 = −5	−2 + 2 = 0

Use the grid to name a point for each ordered pair.

5. (8, 4) E (7, 2) G
6. (9, 1) D (9, 9) B

Use the same grid, name the ordered pair for each point.

7. C(2, 6) A(6, 5)
8. F(2, 2) H(4, 7)

Plot the points shown on the grid. Label the points.

9. M(4, 4) N(−6, −6)
10. O(−4, 6) P(5, −4)
11. Q(−3, −3) R(9, 2)

Spectrum Geometry Grade 6 — Chapter 7 The Coordinate Plane 69

69

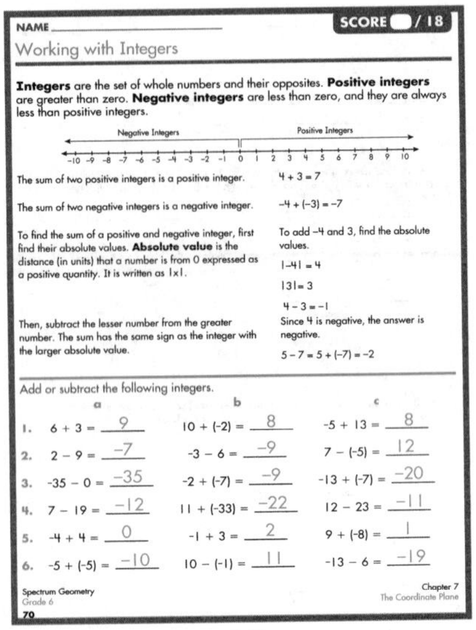
NAME ______ SCORE ___ /18

Working with Integers

Integers are the set of whole numbers and their opposites. **Positive integers** are greater than zero. **Negative integers** are less than zero, and they are always less than positive integers.

Negative Integers — Positive Integers

The sum of two positive integers is a positive integer. 4 + 3 = 7

The sum of two negative integers is a negative integer. −4 + (−3) = −7

To find the sum of a positive and negative integer, first find their absolute values. **Absolute value** is the distance (in units) that a number is from 0 expressed as a positive quantity. It is written as |x|.

To add −4 and 3, find the absolute values.
|−4| = 4
|3| = 3

Then, subtract the lesser number from the greater number. The sum has the same sign as the integer with the larger absolute value.

4 − 3 = 1
Since 4 is negative, the answer is negative.
5 − 7 = 5 + (−7) = −2

Add or subtract the following integers.

	a	b	c
1.	6 + 3 = 9	10 + (−2) = 8	−5 + 13 = 8
2.	2 − 9 = −7	−3 − 6 = −9	7 − (−5) = 12
3.	−35 − 0 = −35	−2 + (−7) = −9	−13 + (−7) = −20
4.	7 − 19 = −12	11 + (−33) = −22	12 − 23 = −11
5.	−4 + 4 = 0	−1 + 3 = 2	9 + (−8) = 1
6.	−5 + (−5) = −10	10 − (−1) = 11	−13 − 6 = −19

Spectrum Geometry Grade 6 70 — Chapter 7 The Coordinate Plane

70

Answer Key

Plotting Ordered Pairs

The position of any point on a grid can be described by an **ordered pair** of numbers. The two numbers are named in order: (x, y). Point A on the grid at the right is named by the ordered pair (3, 2). It is located at 3 on the horizontal scale (x) and 2 on the vertical scale (y). The number on the horizontal scale is always named first in an ordered pair. Point B is named by the ordered pair (7, 3).

Use Grid 1 to name the point or ordered pair.

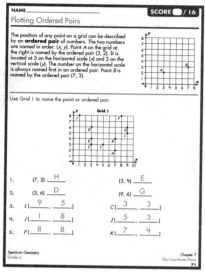

Grid 1

1. (7, 2) __H__   (3, 4) __E__
2. (3, 6) __D__   (9, 6) __G__
3. L(__9__ , __5__)   C(__3__ , __3__)
4. J(__1__ , __8__)   I(__5__ , __3__)
5. F(__8__ , __8__)   K(__7__ , __4__)

Spectrum Geometry
Grade 6
Chapter 7
The Coordinate Plane
71

71

Plotting Ordered Pairs

Use Grid 1 to name the point for each ordered pair.

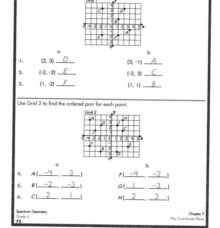

Grid 1

     a   b
1. (2, 3) __D__   (3, -1) __A__
2. (-2, -2) __E__   (-2, 3) __C__
3. (1, -2) __F__   (1, 1) __B__

Use Grid 2 to find the ordered pair for each point.

Grid 2

     a   b
4. A(__-4__ , __3__)   F(__-4__ , __-2__)
5. B(__-2__ , __-3__)   G(__1__ , __-3__)
6. C(__2__ , __1__)   H(__2__ , __3__)

Spectrum Geometry
Grade 6
Chapter 7
The Coordinate Plane
72

72

Drawing Shapes

A polygon is a closed shape created by straight lines. The vertices of a polygon are the points where the lines intersect. These vertices can be described by coordinates and plotted on a coordinate plane. When the points are connected by straight lines, they form a polygon.

The points A(-6, 3), B(-3, 6), and C(-3, 1) are plotted on a coordinate plane. When the points are connected with straight lines, they form a triangle, a type of polygon.

Plot the points on the coordinate plane and connect the points with straight lines.

1. A(-2, 3), B(2, 3), C(-4, -2), D(4, -2)

Which type of polygon did you draw?

__trapezoid__

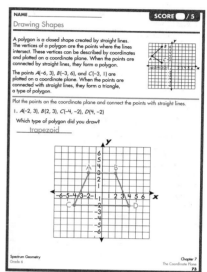

Spectrum Geometry
Grade 6
Chapter 7
The Coordinate Plane
73

73

Drawing Shapes

Plot the points on the coordinate plane and connect the points with straight lines.

1. E(1, -3), F(5, -2), G(5, -5), H(4, -3)

Which type of polygon did you draw? __quadrilateral__

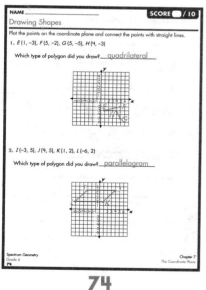

2. I(-3, 5), J(4, 5), K(1, 2), L(-6, 2)

Which type of polygon did you draw? __parallelogram__

Spectrum Geometry
Grade 6
Chapter 7
The Coordinate Plane
74

74

Plotting Ordered Pairs

Read the problem carefully and solve. Show your work under each question.

Irene draws a coordinate plane and plots points to help her decide where to paint flowers on her bedroom wall. The grid is shown to the right.

Grid 2

1. Irene plans to paint a lilac flower at point (4, 2) on the grid. Which letter represents this point?

__I__

2. If Irene moves point H two units to the right, what will be the coordinate location of the new point on the grid?

__(4, 3)__

3. Irene plans to paint a rose at point (-3, 3) on the grid. Which letter represents this point?

__A__

Spectrum Geometry
Grade 6
Chapter 7
The Coordinate Plane
75

75

NAME _____

💡 **Check What You Learned**

The Coordinate Plane

Add or subtract the following integers.

    a   b   c
1. 5 + 9 = __14__   12 − 15 = __-3__   -6 + (-20) = __-26__
2. 17 − 23 = __-6__   -8 − (-4) = __-4__   7 − 18 = __-11__
3. 13 + 2 = __15__   11 − (-6) = __17__   -3 + (-6) = __-9__
4. -5 + 1 = __-4__   32 − (-9) = __41__   6 − 4 = __2__

Use the grid to name a point for each ordered pair.

5. (8, 7) __B__   (4, 3) __E__
6. (1, 7) __C__   (3, 5) __G__

Using the same grid, name the ordered pair for each point.

7. A(__10__ , __5__)   H(__7__ , __4__)
8. F(__4__ , __9__)   D(__1__ , __1__)

Plot the points shown on the grid. Label the points.

9. M(-3, -4)   N(9, -6)
10. O(-5, 7)   P(7, -2)
11. Q(-7, 2)   R(8, 7)

Spectrum Geometry
Grade 6
Chapter 7
The Coordinate Plane
76

76

Answer Key

Final Test Chapters 1–7

NAME _____

Identify each of the following and name it.

1. A _____ ray ___$\overrightarrow{AB}$___   3 _____ segment ___$\overline{RS}$ or $\overline{SR}$___

2. C B D _____ line ___$\overleftrightarrow{CD}$ or $\overleftrightarrow{DC}$___   line ___$\overleftrightarrow{JK}$ or $\overleftrightarrow{KJ}$___

3. _____ ray ___$\overrightarrow{EF}$___   M _____ segment ___$\overline{LM}$ or $\overline{ML}$___

Name the angles and tell if they are acute (A), obtuse (O), or right (R).

4.
∠PQR or ∠RQP   ∠DEF or ∠FED   ∠RST or ∠TSR
A   A   R

Identify each pair of angles as vertical (V), supplementary (S), or complementary (C).

5. ∠A and ∠C = ___V___
6. ∠A and ∠B = ___S___
7. ∠B and ∠D = ___V___
8. ∠B and ∠C = ___S___
9. ∠X and ∠Y = ___C___

Identify the triangles as acute (A), obtuse (O), or right (R).

10.   A   R   O   R

Spectrum Geometry
Grade 6
77

Final Test
Chapters 1–7
77

77

Final Test Chapters 1–7

NAME _____

Add or subtract the following integers.

a   b   c
11. 7 + 11 = ___18___   2 – 1 = ___1___   7 – 18 = ___–11___

Plot the following coordinates on the grid and connect the points by straight lines.

12. A (3, 3), B (6, 6), C (10, 6), D (7, 3)
E (3, –3), F (7, –3), G (10, –6), H (6, –6)

13. What type of polygon did you draw?
___rhombus___

Use the figure at the right to answer the questions.

14. Name the circle. ___A___
15. Name the origin. ___A___
16. Name a radius. ___AB, AD, AC___
17. Name a chord. ___CD, EF___
18. Name the diameter. ___CD___

Find the area of each figure.
19.   ___78___ square feet   ___72___ square inches   ___77___ square centimeters

Spectrum Geometry
Grade 6
78

Final Test
Chapters 1–7
78

78

Final Test Chapters 1–7

NAME _____

Find the volume of each figure.

a   b
20.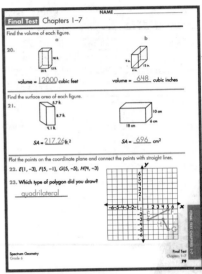

volume = ___12000___ cubic feet   volume = ___648___ cubic inches

Find the surface area of each figure.
21.

SA = ___217.26___ ft.^{2} SA = ___696___ cm^2

Plot the points on the coordinate plane and connect the points with straight lines.

22. E (1, –3), F (5, –1), G (5, –5), H (4, –3)

23. Which type of polygon did you draw?
___quadrilateral___

Spectrum Geometry
Grade 6
79

Final Test
Chapters 1–7
79

79

Final Test Chapters 1–7

NAME _____

Solve each problem.

24. Jayden draws the figure below. Identify ∠X and ∠Y as complementary, vertical, or supplementary angles. Solve for the measure of ∠X if ∠Y = 38°.

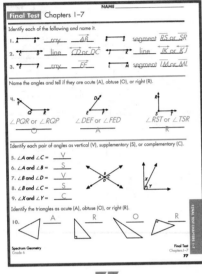

∠X and ∠Y are ___complementary___ angles.

∠X measures ___52°___.

25. Craig's backyard is a rectangle 25 meters long and 20 meters wide. What is the perimeter of Craig's yard?

The perimeter of Craig's yard is ___90___ meters.

26. A shipping crate is 0.85 meters long, 0.4 meters wide, and 0.3 meters high. What is the volume of the crate?

The crate's volume is ___0.102___ cubic meters.

27. A room is 8.6 meters wide and 10.2 meters long. What is the area of the room?

The area of the room is ___87.72___ square meters.

Spectrum Geometry
Grade 6
80

Final Test
Chapters 1–7

80

Final Test Chapters 1–7

NAME _____

Solve each problem. Show your work.

28. Mr. Ruiz wants to put a fence around his backyard. The yard is a rectangle 50 feet long and 28 feet wide. How many feet of fence will he need?

Mr. Ruiz will need ___156___ feet of fence.

29. Andrew has an aquarium that is 16 inches long, 10 inches wide, and 9 inches deep. What is the volume of Andrew's aquarium?

The volume of Andrew's aquarium is ___1440___ cubic inches.

30. A city park is shaped like a right triangle. Its base is 20 yards and its depth is 48 yards. What is the area of the park?

The area of the park is ___480___ square yards.

The third side of the park is 52 yards. What is the perimeter of the park?

The perimeter is ___120___ yards.

31. A paving brick is 3 inches wide, 2 inches high, and 6 inches long. What is the volume of the brick?

The volume is ___36___ cubic inches.

Spectrum Geometry
Grade 6
81

Final Test
Chapters 1–7
81

81

Final Test Chapters 1–7

NAME _____

Solve each problem. Show your work.

31. A drawing of a house is made up of a rectangle for the walls and a triangle for the roof. The base of the drawing is 9 inches wide. The height of the walls is 7 inches. And the height to the top of the roof is 10 inches. What is the area of the house in the drawing?

The area of the drawing is ___76.5___ square inches.

32. A building with a flat roof is 11 meters long, 8 meters wide, and 6 meters high. What is the surface area?

The surface area of the building is ___404___ square meters.

33. An aquarium is 50 centimeters long, 20 centimeters wide, and 30 centimeters high. How many cubic centimeters of water can it hold?

The aquarium can hold ___30000___ cubic centimeters of water.

34. Opal needs to wrap a box. The box is 12 inches by 8 inches by 1.5 inches. If she wants to wrap it with no overlap, how much paper does she need?

Opal needs ___252___ square inches of paper.

Spectrum Geometry
Grade 6
82

Final Test
Chapters 1–7

82